4 × 21/, — 10/15

THE FASHION BOOK

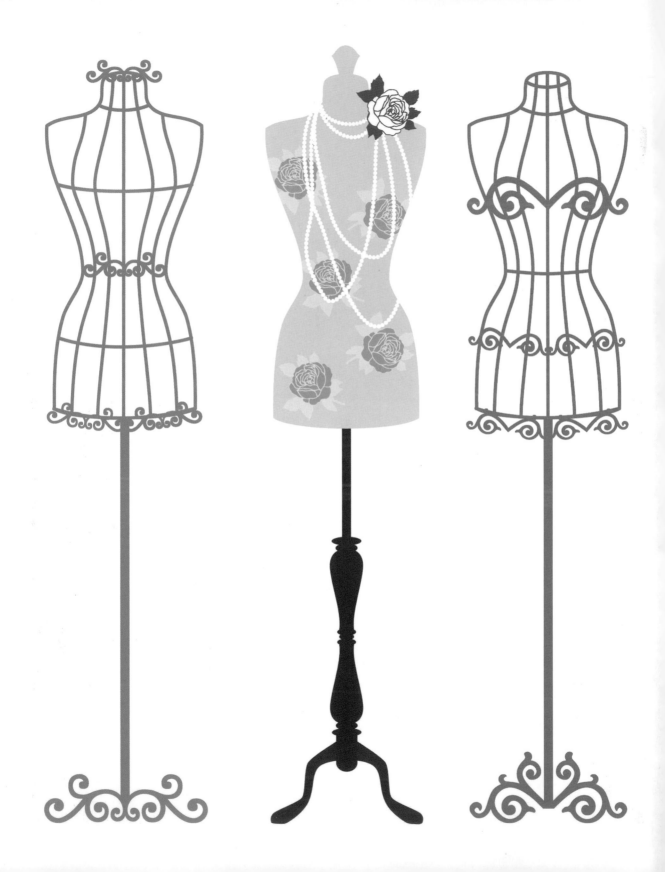

THE
FASHION
BOOK

**LONDON, NEW YORK, MELBOURNE,
MUNICH, AND DELHI**

Senior Editor Kathryn Hennessy
Senior Art Editors Gadi Farfour, Jacqui Swan
Editor Alexandra Beeden
US Editor Allison Singer
Designer Natalie Godwin
Illustrators Alexander Lloyd, Vanessa Hamilton
Commissioned Photography Heather Hughes
DK Picture Library Myriam Megharbi
Jacket Designer Natalie Godwin, Laura Brim
Jacket Editor Maud Whatley
Jacket Design Development Manager Sophia MTT
Producer, Pre-Production Lucy Sims
Repro Opus Multimedia Services, Delhi
Producer Vivienne Yong
Managing Editor Esther Ripley
Managing Art Editor Karen Self
Publisher Sarah Larter
Art Director Phil Ormerod
Associate Publishing Director Liz Wheeler
Publishing Director Jonathan Metcalf

Author Alexandra Black
Consultant Jemima Klenk

First American edition, 2014
Published in the United States by DK Publishing,
345 Hudson Street, New York, New York 10014

14 15 16 17 18 10 9 8 7 6 5 4 3 2 1
001—196338—Sept/14

Published in Great Britain by Dorling Kindersley Limited.

A catalog record for this book is available from the
Library of Congress.
ISBN: 978–1–4654–2284–2

Printed and bound in China by Leo Paper Products.

DK books are available at special discounts when purchased in bulk for
sales promotions, premiums, fund-raising, or educational use. For
details, contact: DK Publishing Special Markets, 345 Hudson Street,
New York, New York 10014 or SpecialSales@dk.com

**Discover more at
www.dk.com**

Foreword

Fashion can be overwhelming. How do you find your way when designers produce four (or more) collections a year, stores sell new stuff every week, and looks fade on and off of the "what's hot" list? How do you establish your own style, rather than slavishly following everyone else? And how do you create a unique look and keep up with fashion trends without spending lots of money? The trick is to use clothes and accessories to express your identity—who you are and who you want to be. By sticking with that identity and making small changes when you feel like it, you can invent a distinctive style that you can really call your own.

It helps to know how fashion began, and how it got to where it is today. After all, most designers are constantly stealing silhouettes, colors, motifs, and fabrics from the past to create something new (those things you see in stores every day). And that's the idea behind this book—to reveal the mystery of how modern fashion works, and to show you all the things that have been brought forward from the past because they work so well (most of which you'll never see in the glossy magazines). It's a look book of styles borrowed from the past and recycled, restyled, and reinvented for now. It explains where many of the things you wear first came from (not just vintage—some of them are thousands of years old). It also shows just how fun fashion can be (sometimes it's downright hilarious), and what crazy lengths people have gone to in order to keep up with trends.

You'll also find inspiration from some of the most famous names in fashion, from Coco Chanel to Kate Moss, and their secrets for flattering and fabulous looks that never seem out of date. And there's more, including the inside story on the front row of a runway show; what fashion will be like in the future; and the diaries of the people who make fashion happen, from designers to makeup artists and models. In short, everything a young fashionista needs to make her way in the dizzy and dazzling world of fashion.

Alexandra S

66 Buy less, **choose well**, and do it yourself! **99**
Vivienne Westwood

GET THE LOOK!

Contents

VINTAGE STYLE

Open

PARTY TIME

EVERYTHING MUST GO!

FIRST EARRINGS WORN IN ANCIENT GREECE, 3,000 YEARS AGO

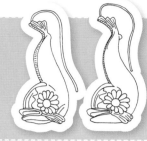

THE MIDAS TOUCH
Gold was used for earrings (like these Roman dolphins), bangles, arm bands, hair bands, and even thigh bands. A brooch was the essential accessory, used like a safety pin to hold a dress on.

HANDS FREE
To stop robes (called *himations*) from dragging on the ground, Greeks flung one end over their shoulder and pinned it in place. The resulting one-shoulder look left one arm completely free for work or activities.

The original goddess look

PERFECT PATTERNS
The Ancient Greeks loved decoration on their clothes—they were especially fond of symmetrical patterns. Decorations were painted or embroidered around the edges of clothing.

10   PINS WERE NEEDED TO KEEP SOME DRESSES FROM FALLING DOWN

ART OF DRAPING
The Ancient Greeks and Romans learned how to drape fabric from the Indians. The idea was to have a versatile cloth that could be wrapped around the body in various ways. Luckily this was also very flattering and suited any body type.

NO SHOES INDOORS!

SUMMER SANDALS
Some shoemakers in Ancient Greece carved designs or put nails on the undersoles of sandals so that they left a pattern or message as the wearer walked.

Goddess Glamour

Reinvent yourself as Aphrodite, the Ancient Greek goddess of love and beauty, in one of the eternal looks of fashion.

This is one style story that is never out of date. Although it was designed 5,000 years ago, the draped, one-shouldered dress has remained a classic. It appears every year on the red carpet on at least one major star, usually worn as a full-length, luxury gown in shimmering silk satin. The short, casual version in cotton is considered an essential item in any summer wardrobe, and ensures paparazzi- (or Instagram-) worthy vacation photos—sun-kissed limbs essential.

Armlet on free arm

Silk or light cotton drape best

Short length to show off athletic legs

In ancient times, bodies were covered in real gold

Get the Look

♥ GOLD HEADBAND gives hair an added glow in the sunlight and keeps goddess curls under control on hot days.

♥ ARMLET draws attention to bare arms. Armlets in the shape of a coiled snake or wreath were worn by warriors, queens, and the women of Ancient Greece.

White   Ecru   Gold   Purple   Yellow

♥ BRONZER OR BLUSH is all you need, unlike the Ancient Greeks who wore so much makeup that it ran down their faces on hot days.

In with the **Ancients**

They may go back at least 5,000 years, but the ancient civilizations of the Mediterranean, including Egypt, Rome, Greece, and Byzantium, were actually pretty fashion-forward, wearing clothes and accessories that are still popular today.

Headdress worn over shaved head

Egyptian Queen Nefertiti made pleats fashionable

CLASSIC ICONS
The jewelry-loving Byzantines wore pendants of the Christian cross and images of saints.

MAGIC RINGS
Egyptian jewelry featured animals thought to have special powers, such as cats, vultures, and beetles.

Sunscreen made from rice bran (still used today)

> " She [Cleopatra] was a woman of **surpassing beauty**. "
> Dio, Ancient Roman

Elizabeth Taylor played Cleopatra in a 1963 movie and copied her Kohl eyeliner

PAINTED FACES
In Ancient Egypt even children wore eyeliner, supposedly to keep evil away. It also worked as an insect repellent.

Wig woven with gold and jewels

BODY CONSCIOUS
Egyptian women wore dresses made from linen, woven so thinly that it was practically transparent.

Hair dye was popular, especially blonde, red, and black

Breastband for support

Early version of underwear

Hot tongs used to curl hair

Lion and snakes represent strength and fertility

Naked up top + Tight corset around waist = Instant uplift!

CENSORED

Hip-hugging skirt

NEVER A BAD HAIR DAY
Minoans always wore their hair long, and they used oil and jewelry to create elaborate styles.

FIRST BIKINIS
Roman women worked out in a type of bikini—far more practical than the one-shouldered tunic Greek girls wore.

Lose your brooches and your dress falls off

LIFESAVING ACCESSORY
If you were injured in battle, your brooch could be used to hold your wound together.

Tube of cloth folded over at top

CUSTOMIZED CLOTHING
This style of Greek dress, called a *peplos*, was woven and dyed to order in bright colors, stripes, or polka dots.

SPARTAN WOMEN WERE CALLED "THIGH-FLASHERS" BECAUSE THEY LEFT THE SIDES OF THEIR DRESSES COMPLETELY OPEN.

FUTURE FASHION
Minoan ladies used corsets to create an hourglass figure (a shape that didn't appear again until the 19th century).

LEARN TO LOVE YOUR VEIL

MAJOR HEADACHE

There was one thing that couldn't be avoided in medieval times—the Church rule that married women must cover their hair. But it was fun trying out different veils.

Wimple wraps around head and neck

Veil covers long, loose hair

THE DAMSEL LOOK

Dresses with high waists, tight-fitting bodices, and long, flowing skirts became all the rage. It was one way around the church law that said women should be covered from neck to toe, though clergy objected to the extravagant length of the gowns.

Sleeve openings are extra wide

ALL ABOUT THE DRESS

Medieval men and women both wore dresses, cut in very similar styles. The main differences were that men had beards and were allowed to flash their legs through a long split in their tunic.

Belt to emphasize the waist

2 NUMBER OF GARTERS TO HOLD LEGGINGS UP (THEY DON'T JOIN AT THE TOP)

STRETCH LEGGINGS

Considering there was no heating, leggings (called "hose" back then) were essential clothing for indoors and outdoors. They were knitted out of wool or silk (for the rich).

Reveal your legs (if you're a man)

PINCHED TOES

Medieval shoemakers seemed to ignore the natural shape of the foot. They first made shoes with massive square toes, then created extremely pointy shoes.

Long, pointed toes

Made of leather

Head band holds long hair in place

Lacing on V-neck line

Medieval **Maidens**

Dressing in medieval times was not as drab as you'd imagine. The fashionistas of the Dark Ages devised some surprisingly modern looks.

If you were wealthy, you could afford to follow fashion, and fashion in medieval Europe was just starting to get exciting. There were new fabrics, colors, and styles being introduced all the time. Eleanor of Aquitaine was one of the main trendsetters, introducing formfitting French fashions when she moved to England to marry King Henry II. Eleanor virtually taught the English court how to dress with style, not to mention how to have a good time. Add fun medieval touches to your wardrobe with tight lacing, long, wide sleeves, and full skirts.

Sleeves flare at wrist

Get the Look

✔ LEGGINGS OR TIGHTS are the base for a tunic-style minidress—keep them the same color as your dress to create the long, lean medieval line.

✔ TUNIC DRESS doesn't have to be as tight-laced as it was in medieval times, but it should finish above your knees for balance.

Indigo blue

Purple

Yellow

Black

White

Slender shoe shape

✔ NARROW LEATHER TIE, wrapped around the waist or hips, adds definition to tunic dress or shirt. (In medieval times, you would have hung your keys from it.)

Lords and Ladies

Medieval knights in armor, damsels in distress, the deadly plague...
If you managed to survive all that, you still had the Church's rules on
fashion to deal with, not to mention the men in stockings.

Two-tone was highly fashionable

BUTTON IT
Someone came up with the
bright idea of using buttons,
so clothes became more
elegant (no more visible lacing).

Wear team colors at the jousting

Display family colors on your legs

4

THE NUMBER OF LAYERS
OF CLOTHING THAT IT WAS
COMPULSORY FOR WEALTHY
ITALIAN WOMEN TO WEAR IN
MEDIEVAL TIMES.

MEN IN TIGHTS
Medieval tailors figured out how to
join two stockings together to make
tights—and men loved the look.

HEAR NO EVIL
The Church said that the Virgin Mary
became pregnant through her ear, and
advised women to cover theirs.

> **"** I pray you **not to be** the first to wear **new styles** or fashions **"**
> ### Knight's advice to his daughters, 1371

Fur trim and fur lining for winter

Low scoop neckline and small bust

OH, BABY
Looking pregnant was fashionable. The plague was killing too many people, so babies were prized.

STATEMENT DRESS
Beautiful fabric was expensive—in medieval Italy, your dad chose your clothes to show off the family wealth.

TOWERING HEIGHTS
The impractical cone hat was meant to make you look tall (the supermodel look was in).

THINKING CREATIVELY
A mesh headdress was one way around the rule of keeping your hair covered.

VEILED INSULT
A veil symbolized a pure heart. If someone pulled yours off, it was considered a major insult.

BALANCING ACT
Layers made your outfit very heavy, so you had to learn how to walk without falling over.

Story of Silk

The lustrous fiber that was stitched into ball gowns for queens and knitted into stockings for kings can be unraveled back to a humble worm.

The story goes that in ancient China the Empress Hsi Ling Shi happened to drop the cocoon of a silkworm moth caterpillar into her cup of tea, and watched, amazed, as a long silk thread unwound. For more than 2,000 years China kept the art of making silk a secret, but traded the fabric with the Middle East and Europe, where it became the height of luxury during medieval times—at one point worth more than gold.

No wonder there was such a craze for soft, shimmering silk in the 16th century; most people outside of Asia had only ever worn coarse wool or rough linen next to their skin. When England's Queen Elizabeth I wore silk stockings for the first time, she apparently declared that they were "so pleasant, fine, and delicate that henceforth I will wear no more cloth stockings."

ALL CHANGE
Although fashion styles in the 1700s changed much more slowly than they do now, between 1770 and 1789, new silk patterns were being launched every 6 months, making it hard for the fashion-conscious to keep up.

40

ROYAL LAYERS
The formal dresses worn by high-ranking women in the ancient Japanese royal court of the 9th and 10th centuries had as many as 40 layers of silk. The layer worn closest to the skin was always white or red.

RICH TOUCHES
By law only royalty and high-ranking nobles could enjoy the feel of silk in the 16th century, but even after the law was repealed, only the very rich could afford it anyway. If you couldn't afford a silk dress you could at least save up for silk ribbons.

MEN IN TIGHTS
Silk stockings were big business in the 1600s. The main customers were men, who liked to show off their calves by teaming short pants with glistening silk stockings. The trend lasted for 200 years.

SILK MONEY
In ancient China and Japan, silk was so valuable that you had to pay your tax in the form of silk.

ANKLE ATTENTION
When high-heeled shoes became a trend for men and women, stockings became even more important, featuring patterns and embroidery, especially around the ankles. Women's hemlines became shorter, showing off their stockings and shoes.

NO SILK!

In Ancient Rome, the government tried to ban silk—they thought women were spending too much money on it, and that silk clothes were too thin and see-through.

KIMONO CONTEST

In 17th-century Japan, the wives of wealthy merchants held fashion contests to see who could wear the most dazzling silk kimono—until the ruling shogun stepped in to stop them.

NEW HUES

One of the reasons silk became so popular is that it can be dyed more easily than other natural fabrics. In the 1800s the brand-new colors of mauve, magenta, and scarlet made their debuts in silk.

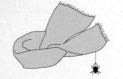

STRANGE ACCESSORIES

This might be one of the weirdest examples of silk—an embroidered cape and a 13-ft (4-m) long scarf made from the silk thread of more than 1 million Golden Orb spiders, which was displayed at the V&A Museum in London in 2012.

SOUND OF SILK

Taffeta, a stiff type of silk, became very popular because of the rustling sound it made when the wearer moved—one way to draw attention to yourself. It made a big comeback for prom dresses in the 1980s after Lady Di was married in a taffeta dress.

DRESS TO IMPRESS

In the 17th century, Italian silk weavers developed shiny silk-satin, inspiring new styles of dress, in lighter colors to show off the fabric.

VERSATILE

And there's more on spider silk: The Ancient Greeks used it for stitching wounds, and Australian Aboriginals made fishing nets with it. Makes sense as spider silk is one of the strongest natural materials.

2,950

GREAT LENGTHS

A cocoon produced by the caterpillar of the silkworm moth can unwind into a piece of silk thread as long as 2,950 ft (900 meters). It would stretch more than twice around the average high school running track.

SPIDER MAN

In 1709, an enterprising Frenchman, François Xavier Bon de Saint Hilaire, made gloves and stockings from spider silk and presented them to King Louis XIV.

Silkworm moth caterpillars are the main producers of silk

Being
Elizabeth I

She suffered from scarred skin and rotten teeth, but that didn't stop England's Queen Elizabeth I from becoming a style icon.

In 1562, just four years after being crowned queen at the age of 25, Elizabeth became ill with smallpox, which left scars on her face. To cover them up, she applied heavy white makeup, and her very pale skin became her signature look. Because she was so influential, the ladies at court copied her, even blacking out their teeth as a fashion statement when Elizabeth's own teeth started to rot.

Elizabeth knew she wasn't a great beauty—she outlawed unflattering pictures of her being made public—but she was able to create an image of power through the way she dressed. Her trademark colors were black and white, which she thought made her look pure. To emphasize this, she adopted the pearl, a symbol of purity, as her favorite jewel, and wore a ruff, which created a halolike effect around her face.

Rumored to have more than 80 wigs

Always painted looking majestic, in a flattering style, with no flaws showing

Owned 2,000 pairs of gloves

Very proud of her tiny feet

Lace ruff at neck

Velvet gown stitched with pearls

Hidden pads strapped to the hips

TOXIC ELIZABETHANS
Although they didn't realize it, the cosmetics so loved by the queen and her slavish followers were slowly killing them. They covered their faces with foundation made from poisonous lead, and dyed their hair with sulphur powder, which caused nausea, headaches, and nosebleeds.

Red worn only by royals and nobility

Fan hides mouth when whispering gossip

Silk painted with pictures of animals, mythical and real

Riding boots for her favorite sport

The Wish List

✔ PENDANT WITH LARGE GEMS: Elizabeth loved wearing pendants—to make her neck look longer—as well as strings of pearls and rings.

✔ LACE COLLAR: Elizabeth's ruffs were handmade, huge, and cost a fortune.

✔ THUMB RING: Very fashionable then, and now. Elizabeth wears one in many portraits (look left). One of her rings hid a secret picture of her mother, Anne Boleyn.

Rocking the Renaissance

To get the best out of living in the Renaissance of the 15th and 16th centuries, you had to forget about bathing, ignore the fleas, learn to love funny hats and collars, and obey (or not) the sumptuary laws that dictated who could and couldn't wear luxurious new silks and velvets.

Cutouts on sleeves show layer underneath

Underdress + V-neck gown + Sleeves = Mix and match

PRACTICAL DRESSING
Doctors said washing was bad for you. Detachable sleeves could be changed when armpits got sweaty.

Simply untie when sleeves are grimy

FLEXIBLE WARDROBE
Instead of a single tunic, you could have several separate pieces to combine in new ways.

1

THE TOTAL NUMBER OF RED DRESSES YOU COULD OWN BEFORE THE FASHION POLICE OF FLORENCE, ITALY, FINED YOU (THEY CLAMPED DOWN ON RUFFLES, PLEATS, AND PLATFORM SHOES, TOO).

Extra-tight stockings show off muscles

MALE FAKERY
Men loved to exaggerate their bodies, padding their thighs, chest, stomach, and "sinful parts" with stuffing.

Bum roll worn under here to give shape

EXPANDING SKIRTS
Women wore big hoops (called *farthingales*) under their skirts. Wider chairs were designed to fit them.

> ❝ Many **scratch their lice**. Some **stink** from their **armpits** and their feet, and many more from their **foul mouths**. ❞
> Girolamo Cardano, physician, 1576

Hair wasn't washed for weeks or months

HYGIENE HORRORS
Furs—thought to attract fleas and lice from the body—were worn then simply shaken out.

Fur-lined coat = no fleas on me!

Mini-me daughter in satin and beads

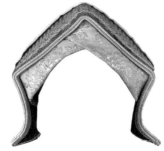

CHEATS RULE
The ideal Renaissance body was tall—pointed headdresses, propped up with wires, helped add valuable height.

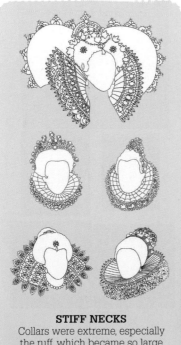

STIFF NECKS
Collars were extreme, especially the ruff, which became so large that eating while wearing one was tricky (and messy).

The silk in this dress from 1753 is woven with 14 colors and four kinds of silver thread—don't even ask the price...

Must have three rows of ruffles at the end of sleeve

A mantua-style gown took almost a year to make

Do not walk quickly (or in wind) or the hoops underneath will swing uncontrollably

Skirt sits over an enormous set of metal hoops

❝ The palace feels awfully crowded these days. In our **formal gowns** we jostle clumsily around one another, **turning sideways to fit** through doors. Most perplexing of all is needing **to relieve oneself**. First, you have to beg royal permission. Second, you must use a bourdaloue, like **a little gravy jug,** held under your dress. No wonder we **pray daily for** the **new French fashions** to reach England. **❞**

Mantua-wearing lady, 1753

Widest skirt in history, about 6 feet (1.8 m) across—almost as wide as a king-size bed

Bourdaloue

What's **under** the **dress?**

Women have been reshaping their bodies for thousands of years, molding themselves into the fashionable shape of the day—one that changes so quickly, it's hard to keep up.

1700s

BEAUTIFUL BODIES
In the early 1700s, expensively embroidered bodices were not hidden but were part of your dress.

1700s

BEWARE OF BRUISING
Most 18th-century corsets used whalebone, but some had solid wood or metal rods running down the center.

1700s

JAGGED EDGES
Stays, as corsets were called, had stiff tabs to stop your petticoat from bunching up.

1880s

WAISTED WOMEN
Pinching in the waist made the bust and hips look curvy, creating the hourglass silhouette of the 1880s.

1895

PUSH AND PULL
To get the fashionable S-shape of 1895, corsets had a long, straight front, forcing the hips back.

1895

Spoon-shaped steel in front panel

HEALTH WARNING
Corset panels that widened at the base pressed in the stomach, but doctors said they would cause illness.

1950s

Stretch panels stop hips bulging

STRAPLESS WONDER
Bustiers of the 1950s used stretch technology, and had pointy cups (pointy bras were in fashion, too).

1950s

MAGIC WISHES
Makers of corset girdles promised to "get rid of your faults" and remove every "ugly" bulge.

1960s

FLOWER POWER
In the peace-loving 1960s, flower patterns were the big thing— some girdles went floral.

> In the **world of fashion**, nothing is ever **comfortable**
>
> Jay Manuel, *America's Next Top Model*

1825

UNNATURALLY SLIM
The long corset of the early 1800s pushed up the bust but smoothed any bumps below.

1875

Need help to lace it tightly

LACING PRACTICE
If you didn't have servants, you definitely wanted a corset that laced in the front, not the back.

1940s

PRETTY IN PINK
By the 1940s, women were wearing waist girdles with suspender belts for attaching their stockings.

Petticoats return but get a short cut

1990s

UNDERGARMENT ON DISPLAY
The corset made a comeback in the 1990s, and this time it was meant to be seen.

FULL CIRCLE
Fashion brought back the corset and petticoat, but not just as undergarments. Now they have starring roles.

A year in the life of a

STUDENT DESIGNER

Barbra Kolasinski is working on a final year collection that will be shown at a prestigious London College of Fashion catwalk show. For a girl who would rather "sew into the night than go out clubbing" it's the perfect challenge.

Barbra Kolasinski
Graduate LCF MA
Fashion Design
Technology
Women's Wear

JANUARY

I'm collecting yarns, braiding threads to make fabric, and hand-dyeing in my bathtub!

FEBRUARY

First sketches focus on line and proportion. My theme is "The Clan" but every piece is individual.

JUNE

My fabric is too precious for tryouts so I use plain calico for a test garment, called a "toile."

OCTOBER

Now I can machine-stitch my first designs. I'm using tartan, with mohair and leather.

NOVEMBER

Hand-sewing is essential for small details like ruffles and pleats. I find it relaxing.

> My heritage and background **inspire me**. I'm very proud to be **Scottish** and **Polish** and I use both as a starting point for my collections.
>
> Barbra Kolasinski

MARCH

I'm switching to the computer to create technical drawings with accurate measurements.

APRIL

I discuss my "look book" of swatches and drawings with my mentor. We choose my key pieces.

MAY

Pattern-cutting comes next. Each piece of the garment has to be plotted on paper and cut out.

FEBRUARY

A 6am start on show day! My collection has to be in perfect order because I'm going first.

To complete the look, I'm customizing shoes with mohair fringe and making bags.

It's London Fashion Week and my designs are on show. Colorful, Scottish, and just a little crazy!

Being
Marie Antoinette

With an extravagant shopping allowance that included four new pairs of shoes a week, who wouldn't have wanted to be Marie Antoinette, Queen of France?

When she was sentenced to death in 1793 for spending outrageously while the people of France were starving, no one would have traded places with her, but before that Marie Antoinette lived a glamorous life as the most fashionable woman in Europe. What Marie Antoinette wore, everyone copied, even if that meant looking ridiculous. One of the big trends she started was a gigantic, high hairdo called a *pouf* decorated with figurines, feathers, and jewels. Some of these poufs were so tall that she had to sleep sitting up in bed.

As queen, Marie Antoinette was expected to change her clothes at least three times a day, and she usually wore each outfit only once. At the end of each season she kept a few of her favorite gowns, and even these filled three huge rooms at the Palace of Versailles.

Hair padded with wire wool and stuck in place with grease

Set the trend for sleeves that look like a Chinese pagoda

Extra-wide skirt (just turn sideways to look thin)

SWEET RELIEF
With no proper bathroom facilities available, the gorgeous Palace of Versailles is said to have smelled awful. The answer was to wear lots of perfume and scented gloves; Marie Antoinette ordered 18 pairs every week.

Marie Antoinette's signature look was bows on everything

Wide, frilly sleeves made her arms look dainty

Tie securely or die of embarrassment

Every new portrait of the queen set a new style

Panniers or side hoops worn under skirt

Ordered more than 30 new dresses each season

Heavily laden with lace

The Wish List

♥ PASTEL RIBBONS: The queen loved feminine colors and introduced a softer, prettier look into French fashion.

♥ SIMPLE WHITE DRESS: Marie Antoinette caused a scandal when she posed for a portrait in a semi-transparent dress. (Wear layers underneath if you copy this style.)

♥ RIDING JACKET: Marie Antoinette wore men's riding clothes, which shocked the palace community.

It's a **Mad World**

In the 1770s, if you loved fashion and having fun, Paris and London were the places to be (preferably with plenty of money in your purse). In these style centers, trendsetters were coming up with innovative creations, like convertible dresses and sky-high hairdos, some of them bordering on the ridiculous.

The more ruffles, the richer you were

Wear it down = Ready to pose • Wear it up = Perfect for walking

Internal drawstring pulls up skirt

OUCH!
After the beautiful stomacher panel was pinned into your dress, you had to move very carefully to avoid pricking yourself.

Pop-up tent for big hair

LADIES OF THE COURT WITH LESS THAN PERFECT EYEBROWS STUCK ON FALSE ONES MADE FROM PATCHES OF MOUSE FUR.

MIX AND MATCH
The "sack back" gown let you transform your look by changing the front panel, underskirt, sleeves, and dress shape.

EXTREME STYLING
In rainy or windy weather, enormous hairdos could be protected by huge collapsible bonnets.

Bonnet shaped like a chicken's comb

Fan for wafting away bad smells

> ## He stuck a **feather** in his **hat** and called it **macaroni**.
> Yankee Doodle

Tiny tricorn hat on a powdered wig

Dressmaker carries a hooped petticoat

THE MACARONI CLUB
In London in the 1760s, a gang of rich young men who liked to dress outrageously started the Macaroni Club.

Puffed out at the back

Floral corsage is the finishing touch

BIG BOTTOMS
Ladies would do anything to make their butts look big, including wearing hoops and pads under their skirts.

LADIES AHOY
Magazines made fun of French women who dressed like sailing ships to celebrate the navy's victory in battle.

Bright red leather

Colorful striped or spotted stockings

LEG EXPOSURE
Colorful shoes grabbed attention, while skin-tone stockings showed off ankles and caused a scandal.

EXCESS HAIR
Attach pillow to your head, weave in fake hair, tease, pin, and add hat.

Practical and pretty hair comb

FACE FRAMING

The romantic woman tried to draw attention to her captivating eyes and rosebud lips. So she wore her hair up, decorating it with strategically positioned flowers, jeweled hairpins, ribbons, or strands of pearls.

31 IN (80 CM)— THE IDEAL PARASOL LENGTH IN 1800

SHADE PREFERRED

Getting sunburned was a beauty crisis, so romantic women were advised to wear a light veil over their face, or to use a parasol—which was also an essential tool for flirting with potential suitors.

LAYERING UP

The romantic woman was used to being cold, since materials like cotton muslin were so thin, and dress sleeves were short. Wearing a short jacket or woollen shawl added warmth without ruining the line of a dress.

What could be more romantic than lace ruffles?

PERSONAL TOUCH

Because dress shapes were so simple and fabrics were often plain, some decoration was needed to keep them from being too dull. Frills, little lace collars, and ribbon trim helped add personality.

Pointy toes with bows or tassels

DOS AND DON'TS

The rule in Austen's time was to wear only black pumps during the day, but (like now) many girls ignored it and wore their prettiest shoes everywhere.

Hair band helps create a graceful head shape

Use sunblock on exposed skin

High waistline

Short, frilly skirt makes legs look longer

Beaded handbag, just big enough for essentials

Feminine, dance-inspired pumps in fabric or soft leather

Modern Romantic

Discover your inner charm with style tips from the dainty and ever-so-elegant ladies of the early 1800s.

Sweet, but never sickly, the modern romantic is a fashion dreamer who doesn't much care about being practical. Her role model could be a heroine plucked from the Jane Austen novels of 200 years ago: a girl who loves shopping, dancing, and discussing boys, but is also witty, independent-minded, and enjoys being a little mysterious. To carry off this attitude, she wears dresses in pale colors or tiny floral prints, and is passionate about finding the prettiest accessories possible—poetry book optional.

Get the Look

♥ ROMANTIC FLOWERS: Roses, peonies, lilies, or violets are the perfect romantic-era flowers for your hair.

♥ JEWELED HAIR BAND: Only very daring women left the house without a bonnet in Austen's time; today a hair band looks just as charming.

White   Ivory   Daffodil yellow   Apple green   Pink

♥ CROPPED CARDIGAN: Keep the focus on a high waistline, and make your legs look longer.

Novel **Dressing**

When fashion rules relaxed between 1795 and 1825, women could kiss hooped petticoats and corsets good-bye. But, as Jane Austen and the characters in her novels discovered, they faced a whole new set of dilemmas about what to wear.

Fashionable green—made from poisonous arsenic!

Fur cap to match muff

Feathers dyed to match dress

FICKLE FASHION
Austen was right on trend when she wrote that she had "changed my mind and… the trimmings on my cap."

HAT HAIR
Bonnets were practical headgear. Austen told a friend that "they save me a world of torment as to hairdressing."

Ivory silk, best kept indoors

Embroidered silk

SHOE COVERS
To protect delicate footwear on rainy days, ladies wore wooden or metal pattens over the top, like platforms.

MATCHING SLIPPERS
Straight shoes, without a left or right, could simply be slipped on to either foot.

SMART SHOPPING
Cotton was much cheaper to buy than silk, making it easier than ever to keep up with trends. But Austen, unsure what to choose for a new gown, wished "such things were to be bought ready-made."

WINTER WARDROBE
To be winter-chic in Austen's time required an oversize fur muff. Some ladies even carried a small pet inside.

" What gown and what head-dress she should wear on the occasion became **her chief concern. "**

Catherine in *Northanger Abbey*

Shawls are constantly being adjusted in Austen's "Emma"

Evening dresses always had short sleeves

Low scoop neckline

High-waisted dress with tassel detail

JEWELRY RULES
Precious gems were for evenings only—they were considered far too vulgar for daytime.

Lizzie wears pearls in "Pride and Prejudice"

PEARL PARURE
Jewelry often came as a parure (matching set) but it was bad manners to wear it all at once.

PARTY PLANNING
Because dresses were all made by hand, deciding what to wear to a ball had to start far in advance.

STYLE-CONSCIOUS GIRLS WORE THIN MUSLIN DRESSES ON COLD DAYS, CAUSING AN OUTBREAK OF FLU NICKNAMED "MUSLIN DISEASE."

PROPER ATTIRE
White was the winning color for evening, as Fanny discovers in *Mansfield Park*; pastel shades were also popular.

Dressing by numbers

Getting dressed in a rush just wasn't an option for wealthy women in the 16th to 19th centuries. Every outfit had 8–10 layers.

① *LOOSE UNDERSHIFT, or (later) knee-length "drawers," plus a chemise, to keep sweat and smells off your dress.*

② *STOCKINGS, to just above the knee, with buckled or tied garters to keep them up, or in the 1800s garters with fine brass springs.*

③ *POCKETS tied around the waist, so you could carry valuables without anyone seeing them.*

④ *CORSET OR STAYS kept the stomach flat and pushed up the bust. Most women wore these in the 17th and 18th centuries.*

⑤ *CORSET COVER, or camisole, to hide the stiff corset or stays, which had heavy seams, rows of whalebone, and lots of lacing.*

⑥ *UNDERSKIRT, such as a crinoline, or pads attached at the hips or behind, to create the latest fashionable skirt shape.*

⑦ *PETTICOAT was laid on the floor, then the lady stepped into the hole in the middle, and the maid lifted it and tied it at the waist.*

⑧ *GOWN this was the most valuable part of the outfit. Fabrics were expensive and everything was made by hand, so a lot of effort went into caring for it.*

⑨ *COLLAR AND SLEEVES were detachable for easy cleaning—they were the areas that got dirty quickest.*

⑩ *SHORT JACKET OR CAPE, often trimmed with fur; this was only worn for venturing outdoors.*

NINE A DAY

To be well-dressed a lady needed to wear up to nine different outfits a day, all with their own matching accessories, to take her from boudoir to ballroom.

① WRAPPER, a gorgeous version of a dressing gown (robe) worn in the boudoir while having breakfast.

② MORNING DRESS, plain with long sleeves and a high neckline; worn at home in the day.

③ WALKING DRESS with a shorter skirt than an indoor dress and heavier fabric.

④ VISITING DRESS, more elaborate than the morning or walking dress; often had a train.

⑤ HOUSE DRESS, comfortable and made of a washable fabric.

⑧ DINNER DRESS with a low neck; much prettier than a day dress and in a lighter color, but still with a sleeve.

⑨ BALL GOWN, the most elaborate dress: low-cut, with very short sleeves, a tight waist, big skirt, and ribbons, lace, or flowers for decoration.

6 chemises

12 pairs of drawers

9 petticoats

1-5 flannel petticoats

9 camisoles

12 pairs of cotton stockings

3 pairs of silk stockings

24 handkerchiefs

⑥ TEA GOWN, worn for afternoon tea, and never, ever worn outdoors.

⑦ RIDING HABIT, consisting of a men's-style jacket paired with a skirt.

plus bustle pads, a cage or hoop, nightcaps, garters, lace collars, gloves for day and evening, not to mention shoes, purses, hats, parasols, belts, hair accessories…

" It is the height of the **summer social season** and **another busy day** for Milady. Since she recently discovered a few **gray hairs**, I've been up half the night boiling **gall nuts in olive oil** to make **black hair dye**, ready to apply this morning.

I wake Milady at **7am**, and dye, wash, and dry her hair before fixing it in the new **fashionable style**, all of which takes a **good two hours**. While she is **eating breakfast**, I lay out her clothes for the day's events. There is **not a moment to pause** as

Milady gets **dressed, undressed, and dressed again** several times a day.

In between **all the dressing**, I must check each of the garments and mend, wash, or **remove stains**. And, since Milady is rather prone to clumsiness, I am kept busy **grating potatoes** to erase the unsightly grease spots on her **silk gowns**.

When at last Milady is **home from the ball** and readied in her nightgown, I slather her face with my **homemade wrinkle cream** (concocted from onion juice and white lily, and requiring much **boiling, stirring, and pounding**). Then I bid Milady good-night, and hurry off to **darn her stockings** ready for tomorrow. "

Lady's maid, 1810

5 HOURS—
TIME TAKEN
FOR A PROPER
DANDY TO
GET DRESSED

SILK TOPPER
When the first shiny silk top hat made an appearance in London, it was such a strange sight that women fainted, dogs barked, and the man wearing it was arrested for nearly causing a riot.

A dandy was always seen in a waistcoat

BUTTONED UP
One of the important rules of dandy dressing was to wear a fitted waistcoat (vest), almost always in a lighter color than the coat, which helped give the illusion of a trim waistline.

PROUD PEACOCK
To create an impressive figure, and to catch everyone's attention as he strode through the city, the dandy wore a sharply-cut coat, left open to reveal the expensive layers he was wearing underneath.

Jacket with wide collar framed the outfit

CLEAN LINES
Before the dandies, men mostly wore breeches and stockings. The new style for gentlemen was to wear long pants that were very fitted around the waist and hips, and reached down to cover the upper part of the shoe.

"ALWAYS REMEMBER THAT YOU DRESS TO FASCINATE OTHERS, NOT YOURSELF."
LORD EDWARD BULWER-LYTTON, 1828

AVOID TOO
MANY COLORS;
A DANDY WORE
NO MORE THAN
FOUR AT A TIME

Boots for a daily horse ride in the park

Ideal shoe shape was long and narrow

FOOTWEAR ETIQUETTE
Riding boots were popular, but it was bad manners to wear them to a ball. Shoes were always polished, but not too much—champagne was recommended to get just the right shine.

A top hat is the ultimate accessory

Miss
Dandy

Steal some tricks from the most stylish men in fashion history to create a statement look that crosses typical gender lines.

It's not unusual today for girls to borrow clothes from the boys, but 200 years ago, men and women traded ideas but never actually swapped clothes. Ladies fretted over what to wear, but some gentlemen paid just as much attention—if not more—to their own looks, and they weren't ashamed of it. These guys were known as the dandies—very proper gentlemen, though slightly excessive—and they make sharp role models for the fashionistas of today.

Wear a statement jacket or coat

High-waisted jeans to lengthen legs

Patent oxfords, must be spotless

Get the Look

★ NARROW SILK SCARF or tie. Wear up around the neck to remind you to keep your head held high. This is the one accessory that will give you instant dandy chic.

★ SHINY HEELED BOOTS: These ensure a confident walk and give your outfit a polished look.

★ CLASSIC MEN'S-STYLE WATCH with a large face—the modern version of the dandy's pocket watch (so you can time your arrival to be fashionably late).

Black   Royal blue   White   Maroon   Brown

A dandy's boots are always pristine

Crossing Lines

Something surprising happened to clothes in the early 1800s. As men and women started to trade ideas on how to dress, their looks became more and more alike.

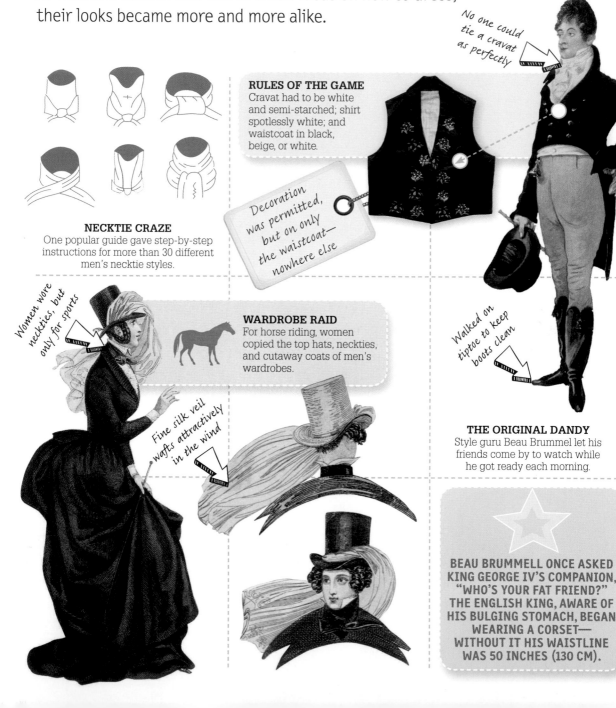

No one could tie a cravat as perfectly

RULES OF THE GAME
Cravat had to be white and semi-starched; shirt spotlessly white; and waistcoat in black, beige, or white.

Decoration was permitted, but on only the waistcoat—nowhere else

NECKTIE CRAZE
One popular guide gave step-by-step instructions for more than 30 different men's necktie styles.

Women wore neckties, but only for sports

WARDROBE RAID
For horse riding, women copied the top hats, neckties, and cutaway coats of men's wardrobes.

Walked on tiptoe to keep boots clean

Fine silk veil wafts attractively in the wind

THE ORIGINAL DANDY
Style guru Beau Brummel let his friends come by to watch while he got ready each morning.

BEAU BRUMMELL ONCE ASKED KING GEORGE IV'S COMPANION, "WHO'S YOUR FAT FRIEND?" THE ENGLISH KING, AWARE OF HIS BULGING STOMACH, BEGAN WEARING A CORSET— WITHOUT IT HIS WAISTLINE WAS 50 INCHES (130 CM).

An **ill-fitting** pair of **corsets**... will make a dress set badly.   19th-century manual

Men's-style watch and fob chain

UNISEX SHAPE
Men padded the shoulders of their frock coats, and wore stays, or corsets, to create the same silhouette as women's wear.

TOUGHENING UP
Women borrowed masculine tailoring, braided trim, and frogging (a type of fastening).

Walking cane was a handy weapon on city streets

Story of Lace

Is there anything more romantic than lace? It is the material of fairytale dresses for prom queens and wedding gowns for princess brides. But once upon a time...

Princes loved to wear lace. Back in the medieval age, men who could afford it wore lace with almost everything. Knights would even accessorize their suits of armor with lace collars, and lace frills around the tops of mid-calf boots were a popular look.

The reason women wear lace today is that they started to copy male fashions all those years ago, by adding lace collars to their dresses. Eventually men got tired of wearing lace, which might have been because women started wearing entire dresses made of it and adding it to hair accessories, shoes, nightgowns, fans, and gloves. In 1840, Great Britain's young Queen Victoria was married in lace, and suddenly every bride wanted to do the same—a trend that has never really gone out of fashion.

PERFECT PRESENT
Lace-trimmed handkerchiefs were valuable gifts. King Henry IV of France gave two of them to his mistress in 1594, then took them back after she died.

MUMMY'S LACE
The oldest piece of lace in the world was found buried with an Ancient Egyptian mummy.

TEETH CLEANING
In the Middle Ages, if you were rich you would have used a little lace-trimmed cloth to rub your teeth clean—toothbrushes came later.

BOOT TOPS
After lace ruffs fell out of fashion, men wore lace flounces around their boots. One French courtier, a friend of King Louis VIII, had 300 pairs.

PAST TIME
Before the first lacemaking machine was invented in 1809, it could take 3 or 4 days to hand-stitch a piece of lace the size of a postage stamp.

LACE LESSONS NO. 1
The best lace in the world once came from Alençon in France. You would have to study for 8 years before you could make it properly.

SPOON-FED
The lace neck ruffs worn in the French royal court of the 16th century became so huge that Queen Margot is said to have used a 2-ft (60-cm) long spoon to eat her soup.

SING, DON'T SPEAK
In the 19th century, workers in lace factories were forbidden from talking in case they got distracted from their work, but they were allowed to sing special lacemaking songs to encourage them to work faster.

SNOW COVER
During World War II, US soldiers came up with the idea of covering their helmets with lace to act as camouflage in the snow during winter battles.

HIDDEN LACE
England banned imported lace in 1662, but fashionable people were so desperate for lace they would smuggle it into the country—with dead bodies in coffins, baked into pies, or stuffed into hollowed-out loaves of bread.

WEDDING BELLE
Just 24 hours after Kate Middleton's wedding to Prince William, boutiques around the world were selling copies of her lace dress.

INTERIOR STYLE
In Victorian times, lace curtains in the living room were a major status symbol—even better if you had lace-covered doorknobs to match.

ALL IN THE NAME
The word "lace" comes from the Latin word for loop (*laqueus*) because to make it from scratch, you use a needle and thread to make every tiny hole.

Threads are held in place with pins

LACE LESSONS NO. 2
If you were a young girl in England in the 1600s, you might be sent to a lace school as early as 5 years old—no math or geography, every lesson was lacemaking.

The first bobbins for making lace were made from dainty bird bones

KEEP YOUR HAT ON

BAD HAIR DAY
Considering hair was washed on average once a month, hats were a good idea—a brimmed hat for outdoors before 5pm, and a lace cap for indoors.

WAISTING AWAY
Corsets made the natural waist an inch or two smaller. This made it hard to breathe, so fainting was common. Grand houses had fainting couches or even fainting rooms.

A 16–20in (41–51cm) waist was the goal

"WE SPEND MOST OF OUR DAY GETTING CHANGED"

FASHION FANATICS
Ladies wore different outfits for breakfast, mornings at home, outdoor walks, horse riding, afternoon tea, dinner, the opera, and parties. A third of the clothing budget was spent on accessories.

Afternoon tea dress

44 YARDS (40 M) OF FABRIC USED IN A TYPICAL 19TH-CENTURY DRESS

THE BIGGER THE BETTER
Flounces and frills gave the illusion of even larger skirts—some dresses were so wide that they couldn't fit through doors. As fashions changed, skirts got narrower, but the bulk moved to the back to make a bustle.

FOOTWEAR ADVICE
White shoes are perfect for average-length feet. Short feet look best in long boots buttoned at the side. Long feet look best in shoes with ornaments.

Feathers in the hair

Waisted jacket

Victorian **Vibe**

Steal the full skirt and frills from 19th-century wardrobes and play with the proportions to create a whole new look.

Some Victorian fashion tips were over-the-top, such as suggesting the fashionable woman needed at least 60 dresses. But others make perfect sense and are easy to copy—wear a hat or oversize hair accessories to add height; match your shoes to the color of your outfit or a shade darker to create a long line; emphasize your waist by wearing a full skirt; and balance the proportions by wearing a fitted jacket that reveals the waist.

Neat row of brass buttons on cuffs

Get the Look

Pearl buttons

✔ CREAMY PEARLS reflect light against the skin. Even cheap fakes can look effective.

✔ COLOR PALETTE of rich, dark colors for everyday and pretty pastels for parties.

| Black | Royal blue | Light blue | Purple | Rust | Orange | Olive |

✔ DAINTY GLOVES for flirting. Drop them = "I love you." Turn inside-out = "I hate you."

✔ VELVET AND LACE: Try a black velvet choker or white lace cuff.

Frills on everything

Shoe-boots with buckles

Exotic Creatures

In Victorian times (named for Britain's Queen Victoria, who reigned from 1837 to 1901), fashion relied on visual tricks—and lots of animal parts—to turn ladies into exotic creatures.

Push up the bust + Suck in the waist = Instant curves

WHALE BONES
Corsets were lined with thin flexible strips of material taken from the jaws of whales.

CRINOLINE CURVES
To create a big skirt, you wore a "cage," or crinoline, underneath, which made your hips sway when you walked.

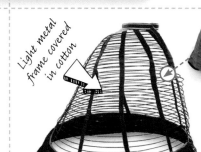

Light metal frame covered in cotton

FISHTAIL TRAIN
They had nothing to do with marine life—but fishtails made you look graceful as you swished out of a room.

Inside, the train is taped to the legs

Puffy shoulders + Slim sleeves = As-if-by-magic little waist

LEG-OF-MUTTON SLEEVES
These puffy sleeves with narrow cuffs looked like the leg of a sheep (called *mutton* when served for dinner).

" Does my **butt** look big in this? "

Feathers quiver beneath the chin

HIGH COLLAR
"It" girl Princess Alexandra started a trend when she wore high-necked styles to cover a scar.

BIRD-WATCHING
Fashionistas liked their exotic birds stuffed and mounted on hats.

Can you balance a tea tray on your bustle?

OSTRICH FEATHER FAN
The ultimate statement accessory. Ostrich farms started up in South Africa because demand was so high.

HORSE HAIR
Petticoats were woven from linen and stiffened with horse hair.

1889

THE YEAR THAT ANIMAL LOVERS, OUTRAGED BY THE VICTORIAN CRAZE FOR WEARING FEATHERED FRIENDS, FOUNDED THE ROYAL SOCIETY FOR THE PROTECTION OF BIRDS.

In love with shoes

Women (and men) have been obsessed with shoes for centuries. Shoes hold the power to make the wearer taller, call attention to her feet, or change her posture.

1600s

THE ORIGINAL PLATFORMS
Overshoes (called *chopines*) on massive soles lifted you above the dirty streets of the 17th century.

1725–50

HIGH SOCIETY
The higher your heels, the more important your social position. Expensive silk added to the effect.

1750

Closed toe, open back

SATIN MULES
Ladies in the 1700s preferred slip-on mules (classier than slippers) since they spent so much time indoors.

1890s

BOYFRIEND SHOES
Designers borrowed ideas from men's wardrobes, like sturdy lace-ups, but gave them a feminine twist.

1905

NEW CENTURY
Women wanted practical footwear in the 1900s, with a streamlined look and modern details.

1918

LOVE MY LEGS
Everyone went dance-crazy in 1918, and skirts kept getting shorter, so shoes had eye-catching details.

1950s

WHAT A HEEL
1950s fashion editors recommended high heels with the new longer skirt lengths (or risk looking frumpy).

1960s

Pointed toe and pin heel

DANGER DOWN BELOW
Spike heels were banned from some office buildings because of the damage to floors—and women's ankles.

1970s

WHAT WERE THEY THINKING?
Designers in the "bad-taste" decade (the 1970s) dreamed up chunky platforms in corduroy.

❝ The future's got a **million roads** for you to choose, but you'll walk a little **taller** in some **high heel shoes**. ❞

Song from the musical *Hairspray*

1790s *Good for one night only*

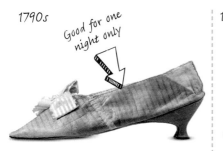

MISS DAINTY
In Jane Austen's time, shoes were so delicate that they could wear out during just one evening of dancing.

1850s

FLAWLESS FEET
As hemlines rose in the early 1800s, snowy white ankle boots became the latest fashion.

1890s *Use a button hook to help*

BORING BUTTONS
They may look adorable, but you had to do each tiny button on these shoes, which took forever.

1926 *Crocodile-leather toes*

THE SPORTY LOOK
Heels became lower and styling was influenced by golf, which 1920s girls played when they weren't dancing.

1930s

ART LOVERS
Footwear designers got creative in the 1930s, making shoes that were like miniature works of art.

1940s

JEWEL TONE
Emerald green was the hot color of the 1940s for clothes, shoes, and even matching nail polish.

1980s

POWER STILETTOS
Career women of the 1980s took to the streets in high heels that looked as hard as steel.

1990s

FANTASY FOOTWEAR
Vivienne Westwood's extreme platforms of the 1990s are now on display in museums around the world.

2000s

ARE YOU WEARING CHOOS?
Jimmy Choo made 5-inch (12-cm) stilettos seem almost normal in the first decade of the 21st century.

Add glamour to
your step with
curvaceous lines

Stamp out the
competition in
sharp stilettos

"Give a girl the right shoes and she can conquer the world"

Show your sweet side in doughnut-printed satin

Marilyn Monroe, 1950s Hollywood star and lover of high heels

A year in the life of a

SHOE **DESIGNER**

Shoe designer Camilla Elphick is creating her own shoe collection in her senior year at the London College of Fashion. Where does she find inspiration? Triple-scoop ice cream and peppermint candy seem like good places to start.

Camilla Elphick
LCF Graduate
Footwear
Product Design &
Innovation

SEPTEMBER

First, I make a mood board of delicious things—like candy, cookies, and my favorite art.

OCTOBER

Market research helps me target who will buy my shoes. They are fun and girly, but classy, too.

A PEZ candy dispenser makes a cool heel. Now we need a mold to get the right height.

FEBRUARY

Pastel leathers and bright patents work well, and I'd like to print some special motifs on silk.

MARCH

My final design is computer-drawn with instructions for the shoe factory to follow.

> " I want to create **beautiful shoes** that make **a statement**—luxurious but **full of fun** and frivolity. "
>
> Camilla Elphick

DECEMBER

NOVEMBER

I need to get some ideas on paper. I spend hours filling my notebook with tiny shoe doodles.

The shapes are right—now for the variations. Lollipop swirls, peppermint stripes, maybe cake?

JANUARY

My mentor gives me feedback— great ideas, but ice-cream cone heels will be too expensive.

APRIL

JUNE

Do they fit? I'm measuring the straps and checking every detail of the first sample shoe.

New shoes! The finished candy-print stilettos are out of their box and they look fantastic.

"So Bad, It's Good!" My debut collection is launched with a photo shoot and a catchy slogan.

AMERICAN ICON

The Gibson Girl became famous for her long hair, piled into a loose bun that framed the face. Women who didn't have naturally thick hair could fake it by using padding and hair extensions.

INSTANT FASHION

Bodices decorated with lace remained popular, but the idea of wearing a blouse was something new. The outfit could be bought ready-made in a shop (rather than made by hand) and was reasonably priced, so anyone could get the look.

Lace trim appeared on everything

MAGIC UNDERGARMENTS

Achieving the hourglass shape (big bosom, tiny waist, curvy hips) took up to seven layers of underwear. The key piece was the flat-fronted corset, while bust improvers created the fashionable, large mono-bosom.

FROM THE WAIST DOWN

Even though the new tailored skirts relied on undergarments for shaping, the hoops and bustles of the past were gone. The shape of the hips could be seen above the skirts' flounces and short trains.

MADE FOR MOVING

Shoes could be laced but boots were buttoned; some styles had up to 50 buttons—adding an extra 10 minutes to the time it took to get ready.

Gibson Girl

Although the "Gibson Girl" of the 1890s was a made-up character, her soft-but-strong look and independent spirit still inspire today.

The All-American Gibson Girl was the creation of an artist, Charles Dana Gibson, reputedly based on his wife—and her image appeared in US newspapers and magazines throughout the 1890s and early years of the 20th century. Even though the drawn Gibson Girl's beauty was almost unobtainable, it didn't stop her from entering real life and inspiring millions of women with her athletic figure, confident attitude, thick and wavy hair, love of makeup, and unique shirt-and-skirt outfits.

Raised collar creates swanlike neck

Hair is softly curled

Simple, slender figure

Stylish buttons

Practical boots you can walk in

Get the Look

★ GOLD LOCKET: Jewelry shouldn't be too showy, and should focus on making the neck look longer (pulling your hair up helps, too).

★ HIGH-COLLARED BLOUSE: Button your shirt all the way up (the original uniform for the working woman) to create a clean line.

★ NECKTIE: The Gibson Girl borrowed from men to show she could do anything they could.

Black	Royal blue	Light blue	Purple	Rust

Crisp necktie gives the classic Gibson Girl look

Social **Butterflies**

Around the turn of the 20th century, clothes were designed for getting out and about—for traveling in the newly invented motor cars, riding the wildly popular bicycle, and socializing at the new cafés and department stores.

Extra-long pins fixed hats to hair

CHARMING EFFECT
Hairdos were so big that hats had to perch on top. Casual little straw hats or more formal feathers were popular.

WHEN WOMEN BEGAN WEARING SHOCKING BELOW-THE-KNEE PANTS FOR CYCLING, THEY WERE BARRED FROM CAFÉS AND ADVISED TO CARRY WATER PISTOLS FOR SELF-PROTECTION.

LEARNING TO WALK
Magazines gave instructions on how to bend down gracefully, pick up your trailing skirt, and walk elegantly.

PRACTICAL APPROACH
The growing female workforce wore a sports-style suit—at least you could walk properly in it.

Beading for a daytime party

PERSONALITY SHOES
Beading and diamanté details appeared on shoes as dancing became a craze and feet were in the spotlight.

Had to be ivory satin for evening

FIRST IMPRESSIONS
Shoes were designed with a slight point so that they would peek out from under your tight evening dress.

" For I've got a **pain in my back** from being a Gibson Girl "

Popular 1890s song about the S-shape

Veil protected face from the sun

Never seen in public without a hat

SHAPELY FIGURE
Lingerie became more important, and prettier, than ever. Key items were long corsets and frilly "bust improvers."

TIME AND PLACE
Wearing necklaces and jewels in the morning was deemed "monstrous" by the 19th-century fashion police.

Perfumed pads under arms disguise odors

Black parasol was best for bright sun

FASHION CONTORTIONIST
The stylish woman was shaped like the letter "S" (undergarment pushed the chest out and the hips back). A padded chest made the waist look smaller.

Accessorise handle to match your outfit

Lavender and violet were must-have colors

LOVER'S LANGUAGE
Secret messages could be sent with a parasol. Twirling it meant "we are being watched"; dropping it said "I love you."

STAGE TO STREET
Inspired by a visit to North Africa, the costume designer for *Scheherazade* put the dancers in turbans. Within a year the turban had become a fashion trend on the streets of Paris.

Scarf wrapped into a turban

LONG, BEADED NECKLACES EMPHASIZED FASHION'S NEW LEAN SILHOUETTE

SPARKLING JEWELS
Jewelry designers, such as the famous Cartier, began making beaded jewelry after seeing the costumes of the Ballet Russes, draped with ropes of pearls and silver and glass beads.

"THE HAREM SKIRT IS A SHAMEFUL FASHION"
VATICAN NEWSLETTER, 1911

SHOCKING PANTALOONS
The first women to wear harem pants on the streets were mobbed and had to be rescued by the police. To calm the hysterical reaction, newspapers and magazines started using the term "harem skirt" instead of "pants."

Ballet Russes dancers

Peacock feathers, an ancient good luck symbol

COLOR EXPLOSION
Tired of seeing women in subtle, tasteful tones, designers like Paul Poiret ran wild with color. Poiret's wife was so crazy about peacock colors, she went shopping in bright green stockings and a super-bright blue wig.

POINTY TOES
Turkish slippers with upturned toes (called *babouches*) were all the rage, for men and women. Shoemaker Pierre Yantorny embroidered his pairs with real gold.

String of beads

New
Bohemian

Express your artistic side with the exuberant colors, gorgeous prints, and exotic styling of a hundred years ago.

Rewind fashion to the year 1909, to an event that changed the way women dress forever. The Ballet Russes staged a performance of *Scheherazade*, based on the tales of *The Arabian Nights*. The costumes, designed by Russian artist Leon Baskt, were like nothing audiences had seen before—risqué, Asian-inspired, incredibly colorful, and cut to allow the dancers' bodies to move freely. Take your inspiration from this vibrant bohemian style, and become an artist who makes her own fashion rules.

Loose in the leg

Get the Look

★ LONG, BEADED EARRINGS: Be inspired by North Africa or the Middle East with multicolored, delicate earrings.

★ STRINGS OF COLORFUL BEADS: Draw attention to yourself with a necklace that catches the light—the smaller the beads, the better.

Colorful print

Gathered at the ankle

Bare feet, or the thinnest sandals

Peacock green	Sapphire blue	Turquoise	Bordeaux	Purple	Yellow

★ HAREM PANTS, in either luxurious silk or soft jersey, give a laidback vibe.

Artful **Attire**

As the sharp lines of modern art replaced the swirls of Art Nouveau, fashion embraced the change—it was good-bye curvaceous body shapes and romantic beauty, and hello straight lines, chic short hair, and unconventional looks.

Red feathers— all about being a drama queen

Shimmering silk, like dragonfly wings

ASIAN OBSESSION
Accessories like this clutch bag were works of art, covered with Chinese-style embroidery and jade-colored beads.

LADIES LIGHT UP
The popular lampshade shape (a flared tunic over a long skirt or harem pants) was first designed for a fancy party.

EXPRESS YOURSELF
Swirling images of nature and colorful enameling made art nouveau jewelry highly creative.

Soft hat with feathers

Is she or isn't she wearing a corset?

SCANDALOUS ADVICE
Designer Paul Poiret said corsets weren't needed under the new fashions. He suggested wearing a bra instead.

> ❝ I freed the bust...
> and I shackled
> the legs. ❞
> Paul Poiret

Wide collar borrowed from men's wear

Wire held hem out

Waistline dropped to hip height

Hobble skirt made you wiggle

Vertical stripes made your legs look longer

WIGGLING WALK
The hobble skirt was so narrow at the ankles that you could only move an inch or two at a time.

OUT FOR THE DAY
Women were shopping and socializing more than ever, so handbags became an important accessory to show off.

1910

THE YEAR THAT PAUL POIRET INTRODUCED THE HOBBLE SKIRT. POLICE COMPLAINED IT WAS CAUSING TRAFFIC JAMS—WOMEN TOOK TWICE AS LONG TO CROSS THE STREET.

Shorter skirts showed off shoes and stockings

TANGO CRAZY
When dancing the wildly popular Argentine tango, you needed shoes with ribbons to hold them on.

Learn the language of the fan, as described by Parisian fan-maker Pierre Duvelleroy.

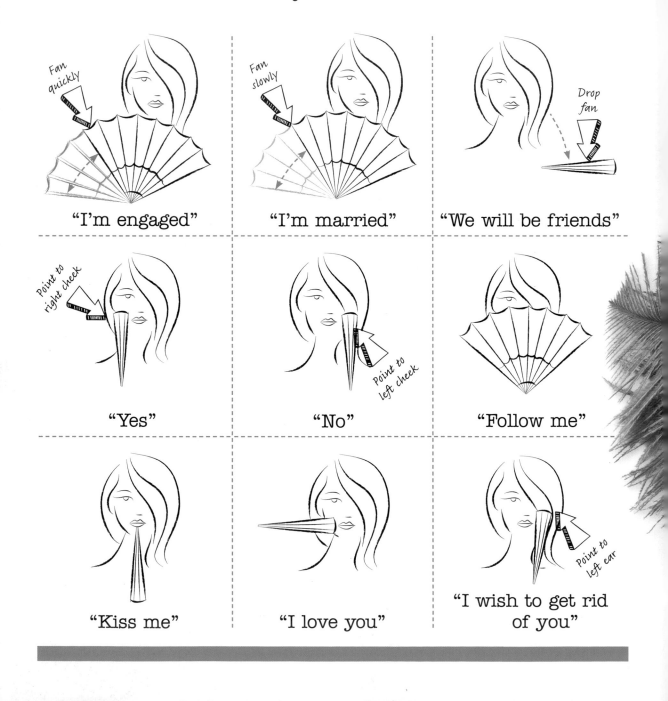

Fan quickly

"I'm engaged"

Fan slowly

"I'm married"

Drop fan

"We will be friends"

Point to right cheek

"Yes"

Point to left cheek

"No"

"Follow me"

"Kiss me"

"I love you"

Point to left ear

"I wish to get rid of you"

"BEAUTIFUL? IT'S ALL A QUESTION OF LUCK."
JOSEPHINE BAKER

TURNING HEADS
Dancer and singer Josephine Baker was the iconic party girl of the 1920s—witty, gorgeous, and outrageous (she had a pet leopard). Her super-short hairstyle and thin, penciled-in eyebrows were widely copied.

Josephine advertised her own hair gel, "Bakerfix"

3

TYPES OF FLAPPER: SEMI-FLAPPER, FLAPPER, AND SUPER-FLAPPER— DEPENDING ON HOW SERIOUSLY THEY LIKED TO PARTY

SCANDALOUS SHOULDERS
Wearing anything sleeveless during the daytime in the early 1920s was considered pretty shocking. A girl could barely get away with it for the evening, and she would powder her shoulders before going out.

"THE CORSET IS AS DEAD AS THE DODO'S GRANDFATHER"
THE NEW REPUBLIC, 1925

SHAKE IT
No more tight waists— dresses showed off the hips, and so did the new dance crazes. The hip-jiggling "shimmy" was outlawed in several towns in the US.

HIGHER AND HIGHER
Skirt lengths gradually got shorter until, in 1927, they reached knee-length—the first time in fashion history that women's knees had been exposed in public.

Fringed skirts showed even more leg during dancing

START HERE
Women's shoes were no longer hidden under long skirts. Magazines advised that shoes should be the first thing you thought about when planning an outfit.

T-bars with curvy heels

Decorated hair band

Simple neckline and bare arms

Fringe, feathers, or beads

Display your knees (tan optional)

Ankle straps and spotty socks

Party Girl

Join the rule-changing girls of the 1920s and adopt the mischievous attitude of a Flapper in a fringed dress and dancing shoes.

The Flapper is one of fashion's most recognizable characters. Back in her day she not only looked modern, she acted it, too. That meant having a job, driving a car, listening to jazz music, wearing makeup, and staying out all night if she felt like it. Though she was far from a good girl, the Flapper's fizzing energy was irresistible. Her mantra might have been "anything goes," but she worked hard to get her look just right.

Get the Look

★ SLEEK HAIRDO, cut close to the head, is the most important part of the Flapper image—keep neat with a hair band or decorate with a feathered hair clip.

★ LONG, TASSELED PENDANT that swings as you walk draws attention and creates an elongated silhouette.

★ BEADED OR FRINGED PURSE, dangled from your wrist on its short chain strap, will give you the authentic 1920s look.

Ivory Black Silver Coral Ruby red Spearmint green Bronze

Fabulous **Flappers**

Living fast and dressed for dancing, young women in the 1920s rebelled against fussy, restrictive clothes. They moved fashion forward with short skirts, boyish styles, and a daring lifestyle.

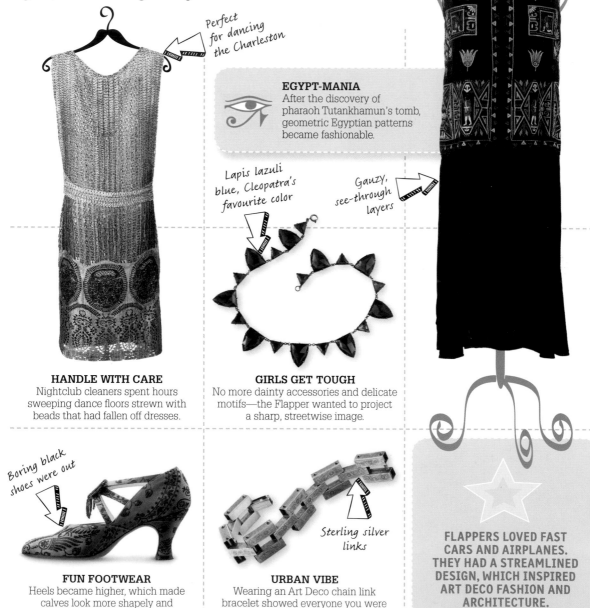

Egyptian-inspired embroidery

Perfect for dancing the Charleston

EGYPT-MANIA
After the discovery of pharaoh Tutankhamun's tomb, geometric Egyptian patterns became fashionable.

Lapis lazuli blue, Cleopatra's favourite color

Gauzy, see-through layers

HANDLE WITH CARE
Nightclub cleaners spent hours sweeping dance floors strewn with beads that had fallen off dresses.

GIRLS GET TOUGH
No more dainty accessories and delicate motifs—the Flapper wanted to project a sharp, streetwise image.

Boring black shoes were out

Sterling silver links

FUN FOOTWEAR
Heels became higher, which made calves look more shapely and ankles look narrower.

URBAN VIBE
Wearing an Art Deco chain link bracelet showed everyone you were a technology-loving city girl.

FLAPPERS LOVED FAST CARS AND AIRPLANES. THEY HAD A STREAMLINED DESIGN, WHICH INSPIRED ART DECO FASHION AND ARCHITECTURE.

"Flapper Jane isn't wearing much"

New Republic magazine, 1925

SO COOL
Forget good posture—the Flapper liked to slouch with hips tilted, to prove she wasn't wearing a corset.

Hose with a Kick

Artificial Silk.
20 Fashionable Shades.

British Manufacture.

LOOK AT MY LEGS
Stockings made from newly invented rayon were so shiny that Flappers powdered their legs.

Hangs from the wrist and jingles

Long, silky bloomers and a slip were the essential new underwear items

Party girls applied blush to their knees

Shawl creates a longer back on dress

DUSK TILL DAWN
New handbag styles included lightweight, expandable bags to take you from day to night.

FOREVER YOUNG
Children's-style Mary Jane shoes were popular because the Flapper wanted to look youthful and carefree.

Being Coco

The original inventor of street style, Coco Chanel turned working-class men's clothes into a chic look for high-society women.

It is hard to believe that a poor French orphan could build a fashion business so big her name would become a symbol of luxury around the world. But that is exactly what Gabrielle "Coco" Chanel did. Maybe it was her rough start in life and the sewing skills she learned at the orphanage that gave her the inspiration for transforming practical men's clothes, like striped T-shirts and sailor pants, into stylish women's wear.

In the early 1920s she started selling her designs—sporty jackets, "boyfriend" pants, sweaters, and loose slip dresses in black, navy, and white. They were simple but looked fresh and youthful compared with the tight, elaborate dresses most women were still wearing (and could hardly move in). With her relaxed style and short hair, Coco Chanel created a modern image that suddenly everyone wanted.

Layers of pearls for major impact

Bold cuffs and bangles (never dainty)

PERFUME REVOLUTION
When Chanel launched her first fragrance in 1921, spraying it around in a popular restaurant, women fell for its lasting, clean, fresh scent. Little did they know that "Chanel No. 5" contained a completely new group of chemicals (aldehydes) made in a test tube.

Wool bouclé jacket— a Chanel classic

Chain inside hems so clothes hang straight

The white camellia became Chanel's motif after her boyfriend gave her the flower as a gift

Right C always overlaps left C on Chanel logo

Black and white or French navy and white

Two-tone shoes lengthen the leg and shorten the foot

Black for sophisticated chic

The Wish List

♥ STRIPED T-SHIRT: Chanel started wearing one after seeing French sailors in them as part of their uniform.

♥ MASSES OF PEARLS: Chanel's boyfriend gave her a string of pearls for every birthday, but fakes are fine, too—even Chanel wore artificial ones.

♥ QUILTED BAG Inspired by the jackets worn by stable boys.

Stretch **Revolution**

Designers came up with some clever new ideas in the 1920s and 1930s. They used knitted fabrics and other tricks to maximize movement and set female fashion on the road to freedom.

V-shaped neckline based on men's vests

THINK SMALL
The head-hugging cloche hat was designed to pull down over newly fashionable short hair.

THE LADY'S WEARING WHAT?
Coco Chanel and Jean Patou used men's undergarment fabric to make comfortable dresses for rich ladies.

Dress looks like separate top and skirt

Silk stripes + Tasseled handle = Chic protection from the rain

SECRET WEAPON
Pleats gave the illusion of a slim, narrow skirt, but opened up (like a folding fan) as you moved around.

All eyes on shoes that color-coordinate with outfit

"I like **comfort**. I do **not** like **glitter**"
Claire McCardell, fashion designer

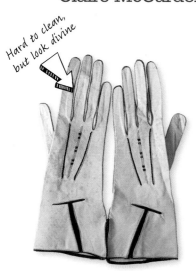

Hard to clean, but look divine

DRIVING STYLE
Wearing gloves was no longer about protecting dainty hands from sun and dirt; gloves were for driving.

THIS FREE PATTERN *Inside*
Miss Modern
APRIL
6^D
1932
Your Ideal Office Frock SIMPLE-AND SO SMART

GLOSSY GUIDANCE
Magazines gave fashion advice to career girls (as well as tips on how to speak to servants).

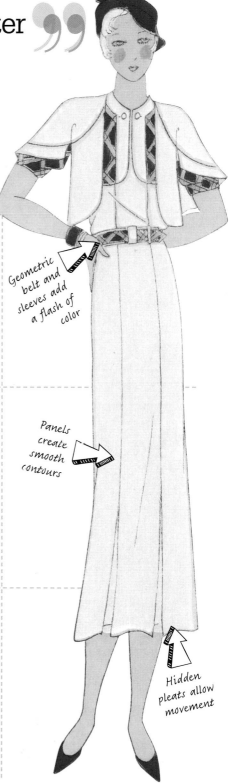

Geometric belt and sleeves add a flash of color

Panels create smooth contours

Hidden pleats allow movement

PAY YOUR OWN WAY
Working girls could afford their own bright, inexpensive jewelry—no need to wait for that diamond engagement ring!

WALKING ON AIR
Women loved the first platform wedges. They weren't exactly elegant, but they gave height without high-heel pain.

1920

THE YEAR WOMEN WERE FINALLY ALLOWED TO VOTE IN THE US. IN THE UK, THEY HAD TO WAIT UNTIL 1928, AND IN FRANCE, UNTIL 1944. (IN NEW ZEALAND, WOMEN HAD BEEN VOTING SINCE 1893.)

Straps form a T shape

CONFIDENT CLUBBING
The T-bar shoe was a must for evenings out—it stayed on even while you were dancing up a storm.

READY FOR CLOSE-UP
Classic Hollywood hair in the 1930s was styled to form a halo around the face, with a side part so that the longer section could sweep around the cheek.

DARLING MAE
As worn by the sassiest star in Hollywood, Mae West, a dress with a daring neckline (designed to show off cleavage) was essential for a showstopping appearance.

"CULTIVATE YOUR CURVES—THEY MAY BE DANGEROUS BUT THEY WON'T BE AVOIDED"
MAE WEST

Flesh-toned with smooth support panels

SMOOTH LINES
With more skin showing than ever before, and dresses clinging to the body, underwear had to shrink—becoming the smallest it had been for hundreds of years. Movie star Jean Harlow went one step further and didn't wear any at all, or so she said.

LEGGY BLONDE
Actress Marlene Dietrich was famous for her legs (they were insured for a million dollars) and was one of the first actresses to show the full extent of her legs on screen (although off-screen she preferred to wear pants).

"DARLING, THE LEGS AREN'T SO BEAUTIFUL. I JUST KNOW WHAT TO DO WITH THEM"
MARLENE DIETRICH

THINK TALL
The slinky dresses favored by Hollywood screen stars worked best on tall figures, but petite women could fake it with the new platform sandals. Dancing stars like Ginger Rogers wore high-heeled T-bar pumps.

Sparkly shoes best for black-and-white film

Classic Hollywood hair, like '40s film star Veronica Lake

Movie heroines wear ivory (villains wear black)

Silver screen
Diva

Learn from the Hollywood stars of the 1930s and 1940s and their costume designers— they knew all the tricks for looking fabulous.

In the days before television and YouTube, the movie theater provided the ultimate fashion and beauty fix. Young women and their boyfriends went to the movies at least once a week and obsessed over every detail of the outfits worn by their favorite stars. Because films were still in black and white, costume designers for the screen relied on dramatic, long silhouettes and fabrics like satin that reflected light and created a glow around the body.

Get the Look

★ FUR STOLE adds instant glamour and acts like a permanent spotlight, drawing attention to you. Faux fur is an ethical choice.

★ SATIN TOP in white or ivory adds Hollywood glamour to any outfit—even when paired with jeans.

Black · Ivory · White · Silver · Gold

★ BOLD PLATFORMS: Working their magic under floor-length gowns, platform shoes add height and ensure a steady walk on the red carpet (don't look down!).

Scene **Stealers**

The movies offered an escape from the tough reality of the 1930s.
Many people lost their jobs and struggled to make ends meet during
the Great Depression. Hollywood helped you forget your worries
with glitz, glamour, and gorgeous gowns.

Frothy Chanel

AFTER DARK
Inspired by Hollywood, dressing up for
evenings was "in." Handbags were
elegant, often with jeweled clasps.

Lobster and parsley print

ITALIAN DESIGNER ELSA
SCHIAPARELLI TEAMED UP
WITH SURREALIST ARTIST
SALVADOR DALI TO CREATE
HER FAMOUS LOBSTER DRESS
(RIGHT)—BUT SHE REFUSED
TO LET HIM ADD REAL
MAYONNAISE.

FROM SCREEN TO STREET
White ruffled dresses, like the one worn
by Joan Crawford in the film *Letty Lynton*,
became an overnight fashion craze.

REAL OR UNREAL
Fun, Surrealist accessories included
a hat in the shape of a shoe, and a
champagne-bucket handbag.

SURREAL STEAL
Schiaparelli used surreal prints and details
like snakeskin fingernails and buttons
shaped like trapeze artists in her designs.

> What Hollywood **designs today**, you will be **wearing tomorrow**
> Elsa Schiaparelli, designer

Diamanté clips on either side

MAKING AN EXIT
Many movie scenes involved the lead actress flouncing out of a room, so the back of her dress had to be equally dramatic—backless, and with frills.

Fake stones still sparkle

LET'S PRETEND
On screen, nothing had to be real. Marcel Boucher created fabulous fakes, using rhinestones instead of diamonds.

Satin-elastic bra
+
New seamless elastic girdle
=
Perfect figure

HIGHER HEELS
Impractical in real life, but gorgeous on the silver screen, Hollywood helped make high heels popular.

The brassière that gives you 'line'

KESTOS

WHAT'S UNDERNEATH
Brassieres were finally called "bras." To suit Hollywood fashion, the backless bra and push-up bra were invented.

HOLLYWOOD GOLD
Evening shoes stepped out with theatrical touches such as gladiator gold appliqué, peep toes, and slingbacks.

FOLLOW ME
Dance movies were a sensation in the 1930s, so sparkling shoes were worn to draw attention to the choreography.

"You are not born glamorous, **glamour is created.**"

Max Factor, cosmetician who revolutionized makeup in the early 20th century

Makeup compact from the 1930s

Lid flips up to reveal loose powder and puff

A year in the life of

MAKEUP STUDENTS

Flora Robson and Poppy Kenny are specializing in makeup. They're learning how to create extraordinary faces and find a way into the highly competitive world of fashion shows and magazine shoots.

Flora Robson and
Poppy Kenny
LCF Hair
and Makeup
or Fashion

SEPTEMBER

In our first semester we cover basic techniques, then switch to makeup for different eras.

We have to buy a complete makeup kit and brushes. It all costs about $2,500.

NOVEMBER

For our joint project, we're looking at house music and fashion. We love edgy 1970s and 80s styles.

DECEMBER

Our working title is "I lost my mind at the disco." Here's Poppy conducting some research...

JANUARY

Networking is vital. We're always looking for photographers, stylists, and designers to work with us.

" Every other person seems to be a **makeup artist** doing online tutorials on YouTube—**it's hard not to feel disheartened**. But we love what we do and if you really want something, you **go all out to get it**. "

Flora Robson and Poppy Kenny

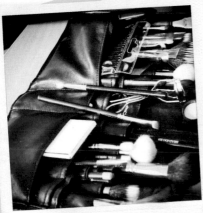

High-quality brushes are expensive but make a huge difference to the end result.

OCTOBER

In some classes we work against the clock because in a runway show you have very little time.

Everything is photographed and checked on screen. (Flora's orange lips are not a good look.)

MARCH

Dramatic brows, smudgy eyeliner, silver highlights, pale lips—and disco streamers as a backdrop.

For the final shoot we create the complete package: clubbing clothes, hair, and makeup.

If you think your makeup bag is heavy, take a look at ours. These go everywhere with us.

PRACTICAL AND PATRIOTIC

In America and Britain in the 1940s, hair was formed into a "victory roll" (named after the aerial trick pilots performed after a successful raid), which kept hair from getting caught in factory machines. Bright red lipstick made a girl feel cheerful and boosted morale.

Rolls secured with a couple of bobby pins

Formed soft curls when rolls were undone

Head-scarves added a splash of bright color

COVERING UP

To convince women to cover their hair with head-scarves or wear their hair up when working in factories, the US government made a film to show how even Hollywood movie stars were tying their hair back as part of the war effort.

RIVETING WORK

Rosie the Riveter was an invented character who appeared in American magazines. She made airplanes and military vehicles, and became a pinup girl for the war in her overalls and head-scarf.

"WE CAN DO IT!"
POSITIVE EXCLAMATION ON ROSIE THE RIVETER POSTER

SAFETY FIRST

Wartime recruitment posters offered factory fashion advice, encouraging women to wear practical overalls for work, and advising that dresses, aprons, long or loose hair, and bangles "are all guaranteed to catch dangerously in machinery."

FLATS WIN THE WAR

Women had a hard time giving up their heels, but were warned that wearing high heels in the workplace would "produce fatigue and falls." Instead, they were advised to choose "attractive, low-heeled shoes for comfort and safety."

Clog-style shoes (not on the ration list)

Wooden heels due to leather shortage

Retro hair made modern

Red head-scarf

Retro
Tomboy

Look to the heroines of wartime for a cute take on a men's workwear staple that has become a casual classic.

In the first half of the 20th century, women were rarely seen in pants. But when the female population was called in to work on farms and in factories, taking the place of men who were away fighting in World War II, they found that skirts and dresses were impractical, not to mention dangerous. The solution? A pair of easy-to-wear overalls. Follow in their comfortable footsteps—short or long, with one shoulder undone, in neon colors or classic blue denim—and be ready to take on anything.

Classic overalls

Cute flats or girly heels

Get the Look

★ COLORFUL HEAD-SCARF: Wear in different ways—twist into a turban, fold into a head band, or tie in a bow.

★ BOXY HANDBAG: For a day out choose a satchel with a long shoulder strap that is big enough to fit your lunch (and lipstick).

Navy	Khaki	Pale blue	Steel gray	Beige

★ AVIATOR SUNGLASSES: Look sleek and ready for action in shades—as worn by Air Force pilots in World War II (though not by the all-female Russian flight team, who only flew at night).

Make do and **Mend**

During World War II, governments issued strict rules about what you could wear. In some places you had to present ration coupons each time you bought clothing or cloth. But style always wins, and resourceful designers and women found ways to improvise.

Fur was a popular alternative to scarce fabrics

Cardigan knitted from reused wool

⭐ WOMEN SERVING IN THE US MARINE CORPS HAD TO WEAR A SPECIFIC SHADE OF RED LIPSTICK (ELIZABETH ARDEN'S MONTEZUMA RED) TO MATCH THE TRIM ON THEIR UNIFORMS.

THINK SLIM
Designers needed to use less fabric, so they made dresses narrower and hems shorter.

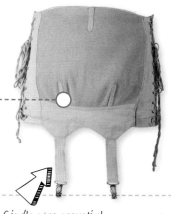

Girdle was essential to hold up stockings

CLOTHING CONTROL
To save material only two box pleats were allowed in dresses; to save ration coupons wool was recycled.

STAND TALL
Although flat shoes were sensible, most utility shoes (only available in black, brown, or navy) were made with a heel.

DESPERATE MEASURES
Leather was in short supply, but reptiles weren't, so you were able to buy an alligator or lizard handbag.

"...take those **old knockabouts** and turn them into **knockouts**"

Advice to American women in 1942, from *Make and Mend for Victory*

Pattern books showed how to make your own "halo" hat

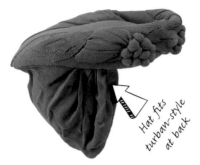

Hat fits turban-style at back

RATION-FREE STYLE
In some places, hat-buying wasn't restricted by the rationing laws, but hats still became smaller to save on material.

STEAL AND RESTYLE
Magazines suggested cutting up your husband's hats (while he was off serving his country) and altering them for yourself.

CHEERFUL CHIC
A plastic brooch was a great way to cheer up a dull outfit, and didn't use limited metal supplies.

Stockings were so scarce that women rioted at shops when they came back into stock.

Small print could easily be matched at seams— less waste

Practical black

CHOOSE CAREFULLY
Under rationing laws, some women could only buy one pair of shoes a year.

Holes stitched up to make stockings last

CAN'T DO WITHOUT
To fake the look of nylon stockings, desperate women smeared gravy browning on their legs and used eyeliner to draw seams.

Change the trim each season

MILLINERY MANNERS

When wearing a hat (which was most of the time), it was important to know the rules. A hat had to be taken off when indoors, unless you were in a church or your hat was small and part of an evening outfit.

"HAPPINESS IS THE SECRET TO ALL BEAUTY" DIOR

BODY SCULPTURE

Dior said "good-bye" to the masculine shoulder pads of the war era, and "hello" to fitted tops with soft, sloping shoulders. The padding moved down to the hips, making them look wider and the waist appear smaller by comparison.

Before   *After*

ANYTHING FOR DIOR

Dior's models were so tightly corseted to create a tiny waist that at least one of them fainted. For ordinary women, elastic girdles promised to squeeze waists in by at least 2 inches (5 cm).

HOW MUCH? TOO MUCH!

The first women wearing Dior's full skirts after the war were attacked on the street because they seemed so wasteful—during the war a dress used about 10 ft (3 m) of fabric; a Dior dress used 82 ft (25 m).

Skirt relied on petticoats and support underwear

WATCH YOUR STEP

According to Dior, "the real proof of an elegant woman is what is on her feet." Etiquette experts advised that run-down heels and muddy shoes were simply unacceptable.

If heel was exposed, toes were covered

Black pumps in silk or satin

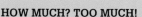

Cocktail hat as day wear

Fitted lace cardigan for instant charm

New Look

Fashion in the 1950s was precisely put together and accessorized. So, if your style is polished and ladylike, this is the decade for you.

You could never have too many clothes, or too many handbags, in the optimistic years following World War II. Christian Dior had recently introduced his fairytale "New Look," with very full skirts, luxurious fabrics, and an array of adorable shoes, bags, gloves, and hats to match. The image of the ultra-feminine 20th-century woman was born; she was perfectly attired and groomed (not to mention well mannered) and always in step with the new styles and colors.

Structured bag with frame— nothing slouchy

The Wish List

★ STUD EARRINGS are elegant and equally at home with capri pants or a prom dress. Wear your hair back or short to show them off.

★ A WIDE BELT, elasticated or in patent leather with a flat buckle, will instantly define your waist to create the "New Look" silhouette.

Turquoise	Black	White	Pink (all shades)	Baby blue	Gray

★ KITTEN HEELS are far less troublesome than stilettos, which were banned in some places in the 1950s for causing accidents and wrecking floors. But watch out—kitten heels can still get stuck in sidewalk cracks.

Flats or kitten heels with pointy toe

Super **Chic**

The 1950s woman was expected to dress up for every occasion, even to welcome her husband back home at the end of each day. With money to spend, and no more rationing, this was the age of top-to-toe perfection.

French style is in

Never relax, always pose dramatically

RISE OF THE MODEL
American Suzy Parker was the first supermodel (her sister was a model, too) and scored her first magazine cover when she was 15.

HANDBAG RULE NO. 1
Your bag should match your size. Petite women shouldn't carry a huge tote; if you're tall, avoid little purses.

Givenchy couture, darling

MATCH MADE IN HEAVEN
Christian Dior sold a complete package to go with a dress—necklace, earrings, shoes, bag, underwear, and perfume.

HANDBAG RULE NO. 2
When dining, balance your handbag on your lap, rather than placing it on the table or floor.

Never ever with bare legs

THE SUBTLE SHOE
Beige shoes were teamed with beige stockings to make legs look longer.

HANDBAG RULE NO. 3
Carry a handbag to place your gloves in while eating (note convenient section for candy!).

"You must **cherish** your clothes
Hubert de Givenchy, designer

Cocktail hat with veil, only worn after 5pm

Held up with stiff boning inside

Pleats draw attention to waist

Small hats adorned with flowers or fruit were in vogue

FINISHING TOUCH
"It is impossible for a woman to appear chic without a hat," said Emily Post, the expert on etiquette and good manners.

1959

BARBIE™ DOLL IS LAUNCHED WITH A WARDROBE OF 22 OUTFITS, INCLUDING "BUSY GAL," "MOVIE DATE," AND "GAY PARISIENNE" (A COUTURE-STYLE BUBBLE DRESS).

STRAPLESS SCIENCE
When the strapless dress became popular in 1950, lingerie designers hurried to invent a better strapless bra.

Skirt almost 3 feet (1 m) wide at hem

TONE ON TONE
Fashion magazines suggested building an outfit of different tones in the same color family, to make you look slimmer.

Carry a spare pair of stockings in your bag

Being Audrey

Long gloves with sleeveless dress, but only after 5pm

Chic, poised, and incredibly photogenic, Audrey Hepburn is one of the most influential film and fashion icons of the last 100 years.

Small cluster, or simple drop, earrings set off short hair

It might have been her European upbringing or her training as a ballet dancer that set Audrey Hepburn apart during Hollywood's golden age in the 1950s and 1960s. At a time when female stars were expected to have curves and sex appeal, Audrey came in with a look that was described as "gamine"—fresh-faced, petite, and, most of all, charming.

In each of her films, Audrey created a signature style. In *Roman Holiday* (1953), it was a pixie haircut; in *Sabrina* (1954), it was capri pants and ballet flats; and in *Breakfast at Tiffany's* (1961), it was the little black dress. But perhaps the thing that really made Audrey special was her compassion—having lived through the horrors of World War II as a girl in Holland, she became devoted to children's charity work for UNICEF.

Layered bangs for the gamine look

Capri pants were Audrey's signature piece

All black is always elegant

BEAUTIFUL EYES
Makeup artist Alberto de Rossi created the look for Audrey's eyes, using pencil eyeliner on the top lid, softened with a brush, and a hint of amethyst eye shadow. Audrey applied her own mascara, but de Rossi separated each lash. Audrey's strong eyebrows were the perfect frame.

Dior's pearls are the perfect accessory with black

Cocktail dress by Givenchy —Audrey's favorite designer

Classic LBD (Little Black Dress)

Dark lenses and frames

Adjustable bow for the best fit

Polka dots are classic 1950s style

The Wish List

★ OVERSIZE SUNGLASSES: Designer Oliver Goldsmith collaborated with Audrey on several designs, including the classic pair she wears in "Breakfast at Tiffany's."

★ TRIANGULAR HEAD-SCARF: Audrey wore head scarves on and off screen. You can also simply knot one around the neck.

★ BALLET PUMPS: Designer Salvatore Ferragamo made Audrey's shoes to order.

Summer **Romance**

Summer vacations in the 1950s meant a wardrobe full of cute clothes that were fun and affordable, and maybe the chance for romance, just like Audrey Hepburn in *Roman Holiday* (1953).

AS SEEN IN...
An explosion of fashion magazines told you what to wear each season, and what to pack for your summer vacation.

EVERYDAY SUNDRESS
Sleeveless, swingy sundresses came in a selection of prints and colors (thanks to newly invented fabrics and dyes).

Hem just below the knee

SUNFLOWER SHADES
Sunglasses were made in new, crazy shapes—pointed and winged frames were particularly popular.

4

NO-NOS FOR TEENAGERS IN 1950S ETIQUETTE:
* NO UMBRELLAS UNTIL 15
* NO HIGH HEELS UNTIL 16
* NO EARRINGS UNTIL 17
* NO BLACK CLOTHES UNTIL 18 (EXCEPT BLACK VELVET)

FASHION FADS
For the first time ever, clothes and accessories were thrown away before they had worn out.

Peep-toes worn with or without stockings

WALKING ON AIR
Girls went crazy for clear Lucite heels made from the leftovers of airplane windshields.

> We're all going on a **summer holiday**.
>
> Cliff Richard, singer

Belly button must be covered

If you couldn't get to Hawaii, you could at least carry a parasol and wear tropical prints

BIKINI RULES
Some countries tried to ban them, or set laws about their size, but by the late 1950s bikinis were a vacation essential.

'50s color clash—brown and turquoise

ALWAYS PEDICURED
Before wearing sandals, feet had to be in perfect condition, with nails cut short, filed square, and painted red.

HANDBAG FEAST
Teens wanted something cute and colorful to carry their belongings in, like the new lunch-box handbags.

BEACH READY
A trip to the beach meant a top-to-toe outfit—swimsuit, robe, espadrilles or sandals, and red lipstick.

Entire bottom was firmly covered

ONE-PIECE WONDER
Designed like corsets, one-piece swimsuits had padding, support panels, and boning for a goddess-like figure.

"Pearls are always appropriate"

Jackie Onassis Kennedy, America's First Lady (1961–63) and style icon, famous for her pearls, pillbox hats, boxy suits, and large sunglasses

Story of **Leather**

Although Stone Age hunters wore animal hides because they had no alternative, leather has since become one of the most luxurious, must-have materials in fashion.

The oldest form of clothing on Earth, leather leggings and coats were worn by the earliest humans. With or without fur attached, leather provided warmth in the days before heating. Then, in the Middle Ages, tradespeople came up with better ways to tan, or treat, animal hides to make them supple and soft. One result was that leather accessories such as gloves and shoes became much more elegant and desirable.

Leather clothing really became fashionable hundreds of years later, when the pilots of World Wars I and II became hero figures in their fur-lined leather jackets. Motorcycle riders and early motorists with open-topped cars also started wearing leather for protection. And because leather jackets were associated with travel at high speeds and danger, they became a symbol of cool in the modern age.

Aviator Amelia Earhart wore leather when she flew across the Atlantic in 1928

RIDING STYLE
In the 19th century, women would wear soft, paper-thin chamois leather underpants to go horseback riding.

COVER-UP
In the 18th century, if you wanted to cover up a blemish or scar on your face, you could stick on a small patch made of leather, cut in a cute shape such as a star, half-moon, or bird.

REBEL REBEL
In the 1950s, when most men and women wore tailored suits for day wear, it was considered radical and rebellious to wear a leather jacket.

5,500-YEAR-OLD SHOES!
THE WORLD'S OLDEST CLOSED LEATHER SHOE WAS FOUND IN ARMENIA IN 2010—IT IS 5,500 YEARS OLD. EVEN OLDER LEATHER SANDALS WERE FOUND IN A CAVE IN MISSOURI AND ARE MORE THAN 7,000 YEARS OLD.

GLOVES ON
In the 1700s, a pair of leather gloves was the most important accessory for a woman, especially if she was upper class. It was considered bad manners to be seen in public without gloves.

THE GUCCI LABEL'S LEATHER JACKET MADE OF OSTRICH LEATHER WAS PRICED AT MORE THAN $13,000.

FASHION SCENTS
The Spanish came up with the technique of adding perfume to leather to make perfumed gloves in the 16th century. They became a hugely popular fashion among European royalty

FINE AND HOLEY
In the 1980s Tunisia-born fashion designer Azzedine Alaia started making skintight dresses and suits in very fine, thin leather, using a laser to cut the seams and make perforated patterns

MACHINE POWER
Sewing machines were invented in 1790 in England by Thomas Saint, who was looking for a better way to stitch leather (rather than stitching cloth).

FAKE

BIRTH OF PLEATHER
Fake leather was invented in 1963. The slang word for it is *pleather* (plastic + leather).

SIZE MATTERS
In the 18th century the ideal lady had dainty hands, so women would squeeze their hands into gloves a size too small.

PEOPLE POWER
When sewing machines for leather were introduced in France in the 1830s, French shoemakers smashed them, thinking they might lose their jobs to the new technology.

Cattle hide is a common source of leather

HANDS OFF THE HAIR

Most girls wore their hair in a high ponytail (perfect for twirling while flirting), but guys spent more time getting ready, styling their hair into fancy quiffs or ducktails (using greasy pomade).

Finish with a neat bow

Don't touch the hair

"THE GALS ALL GO FOR A GUY WITH WELL-GROOMED HAIR"
BRYLCREAM AD

TOUGH GUYS

If you wore a leather jacket it probably meant you rode a motorcycle and were one of the bad boys at school (or the bad boy's girlfriend).

Marlon Brando is so dreamy

PUFFED-OUT PETTICOATS

The fuller your skirt the better, so teens wore up to three petticoats, and sometimes a hoop. For the best effect petticoats were stiffened—one way was to spray them with starch or sugar solution and leave them to dry in the sun.

"ROCK AROUND THE CLOCK TONIGHT"
BILL HALEY AND THE COMETS

AMERICAN SWEETHEART

"Bobby-soxers" were a fashion tribe of girls in their early teens who wore full skirts and ankle socks. They followed every fad and screamed at the pop stars of the day, like Frank Sinatra and Bobby Darin.

12,000
AVERAGE NUMBER OF SCREAMING BOBBY-SOXERS AT AN ELVIS CONCERT

GRADUATING TO HEELS

For the prom or school dance it was time to put on a pair of high heels. Girls could take etiquitte lessons to learn how to walk in them.

Chunky platform slingbacks

Peep-toes and spike heels

Leather jacket

Halter neck

1950s
Rock Chick

What a great time to be a teenager. You had pocket money, loads of clothes to choose from, and rock 'n' roll had just been invented.

For hundreds of years young adults dressed like their parents, went to work, and got married before they hit their twenties. The 1950s changed all that. Families were better off, so teens could stay at school and enjoy being young. The word *teenager* had only recently entered the dictionary, but once they'd been "invented," teenagers were unstoppable—and music, clothes, and dancing became their obsessions. Share their energy with a look that is fun, flirty, and a little rebellious.

Full skirt

Net petticoat

Get the Look

♥ CHIFFON SCARF tied at the neck draws attention to the face.

♥ HIGH TOPS are the ultimate teen accessory, cute enough to go from school to an all-night dance-a-thon. Wear them 1950s style with cropped and cuffed jeans or a circle skirt.

Black	Pastel pink	Aqua blue	White	Red	Lemon yellow

♥ CAT'S-EYE SUNGLASSES are unmistakably 1950s. Blue lenses draw attention to your eyes.

Old-school sneakers

Teen **Dreams**

In the 1950s, teens looked to rock 'n' roll idols like Elvis Presley, and movie stars like James Dean and Natalie Wood, for fashion inspiration. The girls dreamed of going to school dances and proms wearing the new full skirts that showed off their moves.

GLAMOUR EYES
A pair of cat's-eye Ray Ban's (as worn by Marilyn Monroe) added star quality to any outfit.

AT THE WHEEL
You needed a pair of dark sunglasses when driving your dad's car (carefully) because car windows weren't tinted.

Poodles were popular pets—and a favorite motif on purses and felt cutouts on skirts.

Big skirt with petticoat

Pointy-toe stilettos (called winkle-pickers)

CUTEST OUTFIT
High school girls showed off the skirts they'd made and decorated with patterns or poodles.

Stitch on favorite motif here

FUN ALL THE WAY
College girls had a great time, going out dancing every chance they got in full skirts and stilettos.

> **Rock and Roll** music, if you like it, if you **feel it**, you can't help but **move to it**
>
> Elvis Presley

SWEET PETTICOAT
To make skirts full you wore a frilly petticoat underneath. It was meant to be seen when you twirled, so it had to be as pretty as possible.

Dressed for dancing

Velvet-trimmed jacket

ALL-STARS
They started out as basketball shoes, but teens went wild for Converse when heartthrob James Dean wore them.

DANCE MARATHON
Teenagers went to all-day dance competitions, where couples spent hours jitterbugging to win a prize.

1957
THE YEAR "AMERICAN BANDSTAND," THE FIRST TEEN DANCE SHOW, BEGAN ON TV. IT FEATURED ROCK 'N' ROLL HITS, SPARKED DANCE FADS, AND LAUNCHED NEW MUSIC ACTS.

TEDDY GIRLS
Originating in Britain, teddy girls had their own special look: skinny pants, ballet flats, and quirky accessories.

UNIQUE CHARM BRACELET
With charms a girl could mark the important moments in her life and express her personality.

Being
Twiggy

Lesley Hornby (aka Twiggy) was 16 when she became the hottest model of the 1960s, famous for her boyish-meets-baby-doll style.

Before Twiggy, the whole model look was different. Magazines wanted sophisticated girls with long hair or a sharp geometric bob, and foundation caked on to cover the skin.

So here comes Twiggy in 1966, a stick-thin teen who made her own clothes because she couldn't afford to shop at boutiques. Her boyfriend thought she could be a model and took her to a smart hairdresser who chopped her hair short.

Then she looked boyish, but because she had a doll-like face and freckles, and wore three pairs of false eyelashes, she had a fresh new style. All the fashion magazines wanted to put her on their covers. Her secret was to show off two things—her long legs and her big Bambi eyes—and keep everything else perfectly plain.

IT'S ALL ABOUT THE EYES
Apply eyeliner to upper lids, adding a cat's-eye flick at the outer corners. Under the eye, carefully draw in little extra eyelashes in between real lashes. Add false eyelashes or apply three coats of mascara (feel free to let it clump).

A-line shape keeps focus on the legs, not the waist

Plastic accessories add a space-age vibe

Striking stripes add style

Big earrings draw attention to eyes

Tall neck balances sassy cutout mini

Clean, simple A-line shape

The Wish List

★ TUCK SHORT HAIR behind the ears or pull long hair back into a neat bun.

Detail from a Pucci velvet handbag

★ MINI DRESS, straight or A-line, covers the cleavage and hangs loosely around the waist. As short as you dare—all the attention is on your legs.

★ BARE LEGS or pale tights with low-heeled shoes or long boots.

Knee-high boots, perfect with a mini

Mini **Madness**

In the 1960s clothes were fab and fun. Girls stopped dressing like their mothers and joined a style revolution—gear made from space-age vinyl and plastic, and hemlines that soared to dizzy heights.

Bubble shapes + High-energy colors = Far-out under disco lights

PLASTIC CLOTHES
These made you sweat—no wonder deodorant sales boomed in the 1960s.

Cheap price tag, and waterproof

PSYCHEDELIC PURSE
Teens rebelled against anything boring. They loved clashing colors and dreamlike patterns.

Inspired by Pop artist Andy Warhol

PLASTIC FANTASTIC
After the Moon landing in 1969, fashionistas went crazy for space-age accessories shaped like the planets.

THE SET LOOK
A must-have: shiny zip-up mini made from PVC (like patent leather but actually plastic).

Wipe-clean plastic

PAPER UNDIES
Wear once and throw away. Fashion writers predicted that, in the future, we would all wear paper clothes.

THE SOUPER DRESS
Made of paper and printed with soup tins, this mini was a sellout special offer from Campbell's soup.

BRIGHT BOOTS
Head-turning colors, like these custard yellow Mary Quant boots, let the feet do all the talking.

> ❝ Nothing happened in the **sixties** except that we all dressed up. ❞
> John Lennon, Beatle

MELLOW YELLOW
Colors of the decade were optimistic and fun—yellow, red, and orange—or space-age silver and white.

by Wolsey

ALL ABOUT LEGS
As hemlines rose, pantyhose, or tights, replaced stockings and became an essential part of the look.

SOME SCHOOLS—AND EVEN ENTIRE NATIONS—TRIED TO BAN MINISKIRTS.

MINI   MIDI   MAXI
After the mini, and the micro-mini of 1969, came the midi and the maxi. Most girls had some of each.

Low-heeled pumps to match tights

Extremely **Glam**

There was nothing boring or minimalist about 1970s fashion—everything was bright, shiny, and taken to extremes. Dresses were long, shoes were high, and colors were loud.

Dress comes with matching head-scarf

Gold with coral love hearts

SUPER-ACCESSORIZE ME
Every wardrobe needed at least one hat, bag, or shoe made from plush velvet, or velveteen (fake velvet).

GLITTER AND SHINE
Disco music required glitzy accessories that would shine under the dance floors' disco lights.

ONLY IF YOU DARE
The hot pants trend went viral—one airline even dressed its flight attendants in teeny orange shorts.

Chocolate brown and flowery—classic '70s

SCARY FLARES
Flared pants (called *bell bottoms*) kept expanding. Extreme versions, 18 in (46 cm) wide at the bottom, were called *elephant legs*.

Pants must touch the ground (wear platforms)

HIPPY CHIC
Long dresses were not just for evenings. They were worn day and night, everywhere and anywhere!

"Voyage into the **New World** of Fashion "
Vogue, 1971

Zany boots earn fashion stripes

BAD TASTE IS IN
There were no rules about what did or didn't work. No one was too shy to try wacky boots.

1976

SWEDISH POP GROUP ABBA RELEASED THE SMASH HIT "DANCING QUEEN." THE WHITE SATIN EVENING PAJAMAS WORN BY THE SINGERS BECAME HOT DISCO OUTFITS.

Diana Ross checks off the "queen of the dance floor" checklist: purple Lycra, turban, coral nails, and pink feather boa

100% synthetic— watch out for static electricity

KALEIDOSCOPE COLOR
Orange reigned supreme, especially when it came to accessories. There was no such thing as a plain handbag.

WALKING TALL
Pants were wide and dresses were long, and the only shoes that worked with them were platforms.

Theatrical makeup for a night out

SHOCK VALUE
The idea behind the punk look was to use violent colored makeup and hair to look as unnatural as possible. Punks showed everyone they had no intention of fitting into normal society.

London punks (Vivienne Westwood in red)

DO IT YOURSELF
Punk fashion wasn't available in chain stores. There were a few small boutiques selling items, but most punks bought the basics and customized them at home, adding rips, cuts, badges, and safety pins.

METAL WORK
Studded belts and spiked wristbands or chokers were another way of looking aggressive. Piercings were a sign of rebellion, too (although punks borrowed the idea from peace-loving hippies coming back from India).

DRESSING UP
Punks hated flared jeans, which to them symbolized "hippy losers." But in the early days of punk, it was hard to find straight leg jeans, so punks became good at slashing, sewing, and remodeling flared jeans into skinnies.

The taller your boots, the shorter your jeans

Studded belt showed you were tough

8

HOLES IN THE ORIGINAL PUNK DR. MARTENS— THE BLACK 4660

WORKING BOOTS
So, what were punks so angry about? They thought working class young people didn't have enough opportunities in life. So they chose Dr. Martens, a work boot usually worn in factories, to represent how they felt.

Distinctive yellow stitching

Colored hair,
if you dare

Customized
T-shirt

Punk Spirit

You don't have to be angry to take on the punk look, but it definitely helps to have attitude. Here's how it all began.

Before punk fashion came punk music, a reaction against the "love and peace" hippies of the 1960s. While most people in the 1970s were wearing flared jeans and colored shirts, punk musicians, with their raw, aggressive style, were into "stovepipe" jeans and torn T-shirts. Their sound spread from New York to London, where punk fashion finally took off thanks to super-stylists Malcolm McLaren and Vivienne Westwood.

Bag with
stud details

Get the Look

★ WIDE LEATHER WRISTBAND—wear with sleeveless tops for maximum effect.

★ SAFETY PINS are the ultimate tool for customizing; they can hold an outfit together, and add fierce decorative touches.

| Bleached denim | Blue | White | Red | Black |

★ SPIKE RINGS look fierce but are just for show. Wear one or several to show off your rebellious side.

Ripped and
bleached
jeans

Heavy-duty
stomping
boots

Story of Denim

Jeans were made famous by American cowboys and rock stars—and are now worn by just about everyone on the planet—but the legend of denim goes way back.

It is thought that the name "denim" comes from the French *Serge de Nimes*, a fabric used from the 1600s in Europe for practical farm clothes and furnishings. But it wasn't until 1873 that denim really took off, after US businessman Levi Strauss, along with tailor Jacob Davis, made the first pair of jeans using small copper rivets to strengthen the seams. At first, jeans were worn by men doing hard manual labor, like cowboys and railroad builders, because denim lasted longer than other materials. By the 1930s jeans had started to become fashionable, partly thanks to cowboy movies. And when rock star Elvis Presley and Hollywood cool guys James Dean and Marlon Brando made their debuts wearing jeans in the 1950s, denim became the ultimate sign of youth and rebellion.

Long-lasting copper rivets

MOST OF THE WORLD'S POPULATION WEAR DENIM AT LEAST THREE DAYS A WEEK, ACCORDING TO *GLOBAL LIFESTYLE MONITOR 2008.*

TIGHT FIT
Marilyn Monroe was one of the first women to make tight jeans fashionable in the early 1950s. She would buy a men's pair from an Army-Navy surplus store, go into the ocean to get them completely drenched, then lie in the sun until they dried on her like a second skin.

THE FIRST JEANS
In the early days, jeans were actually called "waist overalls" because they resembled overalls, but instead of going over the upper body, they only stretched from the waist down.

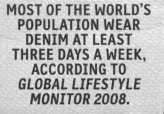

DENIM PROTEST
The people of Belarus in Eastern Europe started what they called a "Jeans Revolution" in 2005, protesting that the elections for president were not held fairly. The public adopted a denim shirt as their flag, as a sign of freedom.

LABEL LUST
Jeans were almost impossible to buy in Russia when it was part of the very strictly run communist Soviet Union, from 1922 until 1991. Young Russians would beg visiting tourists to sell theirs, or buy them from smugglers, but only if they had an American brand name on the back pocket.

LOVE AT FIRST SIGHT
During, and after, World War II, many Europeans and Asians saw jeans for the first time—being worn by off-duty American soldiers—sparking huge demand. In Britain, for example, crowds of teenagers would wait on the docks for American ships to come in and try to buy jeans from the marines as they stepped onshore.

1954

ZIPPED JEANS
The first denim jeans with a zipper were launched by Levi Strauss in 1954. Before then all jeans had a button closing.

TEENAGE REBELLION
Jeans were banned in some US high schools in the 1950s. But by 1958, according to a newspaper report of the time, about 90 percent of teens were wearing jeans everywhere, "except bed and church."

DESIGNER DENIM
In the early 1990s, Gianni Versace became the first designer to use denim in a haute couture collection. He paired denim shirts with long evening skirts made from very expensive silk and lace, and put cropped denim jackets over lavish ball gowns. Each outfit was worth tens of thousands of dollars.

FIRST BOYFRIENDS
Before the first women's jeans were made in 1934, women borrowed from their husbands or brothers—the original "boyfriend" jeans.

DIAMOND DELIGHT
The most expensive pair of jeans in the world cost $1.3 million; the back pocket is encrusted with 15 massive diamonds. They were a one-off pair sold to a mystery buyer in 2008 by Los Angeles-based brand Secret Circus.

DENIM DREAMS
One hotel in Frankfurt, Germany, decorated its rooms in denim— from denim-patchwork carpet to distressed denim-look wallpaper, blue-jeans bedspreads and pillows to denim-effect bathrooms.

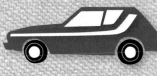

JEANSMOBILE
In 1974 American Motors launched a Levi's car fitted with denim-look seats, complete with orange stitching and the Levi's red tab.

SURROUNDED BY DENIM
One interior design trend of the 1880s was to use blue denim to cover walls and upholster furniture, as a canopy on four-poster beds, or for tablecloths.

ORIGINAL BLUES
Denim's blue color originally came from a dye called *indigo*, which was made from tropical plants. For hundreds of years it was the most popular natural dye because it affixed to fabric so easily, but most denim today is made using much cheaper artificial dye.

Fermented and compressed indigo leaves look like rock

Being Madonna

She ruled the pop charts for 30 years and still surprises her fans, but Madonna's real talent is using the power of fashion to keep her image fresh.

Madonna has been called the "queen of reinvention" because every time she released a music video, she created a new look. She ruled street fashion in the 1980s, setting the trends that teenagers followed—at a time when mainstream dress styles were conservative, either inspired by Princess Diana or the power-suited career girl.

In her early career, Madonna mixed different styles to create a unique identity. Her signature look combined Victorian Gothic, ballet wear, and neon; her wardrobe featured crop tops, leggings, studded and rubber accessories, corsets, crucifix necklaces, fishnet tights, and bandanas. Although she started out wearing cheap, throwaway clothes—known as the "trashy" look—Madonna later turned to designers such as Dolce & Gabbana and Jean Paul Gaultier.

PERFECT BROWS
Madonna refused to let anyone pluck her eyebrows, until her fashion photographer friend Steven Meisel said he hated them. After that she asked makeup guru Francois Nars to reshape them into a thinner style.

Back-combed bangs and oversize hair bow

Cropped layers

Stretch skirt with Keith Haring pop art print

Gaultier sequined cone bra

Short rah-rah skirt

Cropped leggings

Men's wear stripes with showgirl fringing

Crucifix and rosary beads (first one was from Grandma)

Fingerless gloves

The Wish List

★ RUBBER WRISTBANDS: Madonna was working this look well before it became mainstream, stacking them on together with chain bracelets.

★ BLACK LEGGINGS: The essential item in Madonna's wardrobe—either full-length or cropped, with a mini tube skirt or skater skirt layered on top.

★ COTTON BANDANA: Perfect for creating a current version of the classic Madonna hairstyle— tie around big hair for an authentic 1980s look.

Power **Dressing**

Being strong in the 1980s meant fighting your way to a promotion at work, and getting seriously fit. Fashion designers and sportswear brands leapt into action to make clothes to match.

Pastel-colored leg warmers, scrunched and layered

FIERCE ACCESSORIES
Black leather and silver chainmail was a tough combination, ideal for the urban warrior woman.

Extra-wide neckline for shoulder exposure

LADIES IN LEOTARDS
Actress and fitness guru Jane Fonda showed women how to dress for gym classes with '80s style.

DANCE FANTASTIC
The sweats and ballet clothes worn in the movie *Flashdance* became a massive trend.

POWER BRACELETS
Bold gold cuffs that made a statement were the perfect accessory for the 1980s superwoman.

FIGURE-HUGGING
To show off the results of all that exercise, dresses became tight and body-conscious.

SNEAKER FREAK
Everyone wore fresh new white sports shoes, like hip-hop stars Run-DMC. Sweat bands completed the look.

> You want to be **taken seriously**, you need **serious hair**
> Tess McGill in the movie *Working Girl*

Padded shoulders = I am powerful

Blue sapphires— Princess Diana's favorite

FORGET DAINTY
A gold and pearl necklace gave you the rich-girl look. The bigger it was, the better.

MAKING IT BIG
Serious earrings showed that you were dressing strictly for business.

Career girl's dream tote (has to be tan)

STATUS BAG
A very expensive handbag (preferably Hermès) let everyone know how successful you were.

Straight, knee-length skirt—the office uniform

1985

THE MOST POPULAR TV SHOW IN AMERICA WAS "DYNASTY." FULL OF GLAMOUROUS FASHION AND CATFIGHTS BETWEEN THE FEMALE CHARACTERS, IT SPARKED WORLDWIDE FASHION TRENDS.

Heels with powerful points

SHE'S BAD
Super-sharp stilettos with pointy toes looked dangerous—perfect for scaring your male coworkers.

Story of a **Bag**

Ever since pockets fell out of fashion, women have been toting their necessities in purses, pouches, clutches, shoulder bags, and more, all designed to match the clothes and lifestyle of the time.

Late 1700s

SWEET AND SIMPLE
In the days when women only carried coins and keys, a little pouch was all that was needed.

Early 1800s

Hold it in the middle

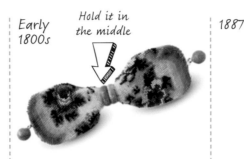

CAREFUL SHOPPER
This 19th-century miser's purse has separate compartments for silver and gold coins, to avoid mix-ups.

1887

PLUSH PURSE
By the 1880s bags were bigger, since women spent more time shopping, socializing, and traveling.

1940s

KEEPING UP APPEARANCES
In the war-torn 1940s, leather was scarce, but imitation suede could fake the look of luxury.

1950s

Perfect for cosmetics

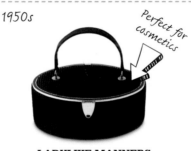

LADYLIKE MANNERS
A structured handbag masquerading as a vanity case could give any outfit a sophisticated look.

1960s

WILD THING
Leopard print was a major trend of the 1960s, used for coats, scarves, knee-high boots, and bags.

1980s

GO GOLD AND BOLD
In the glitzy 1980s, gold, black, and sequins were the essential fashion ingredients for evening.

1980s

Plastic chainmail

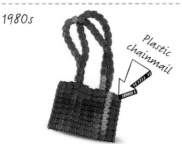

NIGHTS IN ARMOUR
Designer Paco Rabanne reinvented medieval chain mail by using hundreds of plastic disks linked with metal rings.

1980s

SPORT DELUXE
Rucksacks had a makeover in the 1980s. No longer just for hiking and biking, they were high-fashion accessories.

"It's just a **little bag**, but we feel **naked** in public **without it**.

Carrie in the movie *Sex and the City*

1919

HAND CANDY
Popular in the early 1900s, this tiny finger purse was designed to be dangled from one finger.

1930s

EXPRESS YOURSELF
Designers turned to art for inspiration in the 1930s, making handbags that were statement accessories.

1940s

A different kind of mobile phone

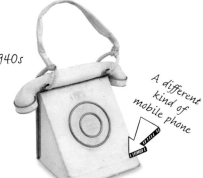

TELEPHONE TOTE
A Surrealist bag was guaranteed to turn heads and show a sense of humor.

1960s

STAR QUALITY
The Hermès "Kelly" was named after actress Grace Kelly, who fell in love with it when it was used in one of her films.

1960s

The legendary double G logo

GORGEOUS GUCCI
Gucci was one of the glamour brands of the 1960s, toted by film stars and US First Lady Jacqueline Kennedy.

1970s

COLOR EXPLOSION
Italian brand Pucci's vivid abstract patterns were right in tune with the mood of the 1960s and 1970s.

1980s–90s

DESPERATE FOR A BIRKIN
Named after actress Jane Birkin, the Hermès "Birkin" had a waiting list of several years in the 1980s and 1990s.

1990s

THE REAL THING
Louis Vuitton bags have been the most counterfeited luxury item in the world since the 1980s and 1990s.

1999

CHRISTIAN DIOR'S CULT BAG
The "Saddle," designed by John Galliano in 1999, was based on an old-fashioned horseback-rider's saddlebag.

SLACKER STYLE

For rock festivals and all-night raves, a beanie was an essential item—for warmth, and to help cover up greasy, unwashed hair (grunge fans cared more about the music than the look).

LUXURY GRUNGE

Marc Jacobs picked up on the grunge trend and turned it into expensive high fashion in his 1993 collection for Perry Ellis. The department store buyers hated it, and Marc was fired.

High price tag—plaid shirts are made of silk

HOBO CHIC

Layering was the key to the look, and grunge superbands Nirvana and Pearl Jam set the trend: vintage band T-shirt, plaid shirt, thrift-shop cardigan, fingerless gloves, and oversize jacket.

"GRUNGE IS... THE WAY WE DRESS WHEN WE HAVE NO MONEY."
JEAN PAUL GAULTIER, DESIGNER

BAGGY PANTS

Cargo pants, roomy corduroys, or low-waisted, ripped jeans were the base for the Seattle grunge look. The same pair could be worn for days (or even weeks) on end.

COMBAT BOOTS WERE CHEAP AND SURVIVED MUDDY FESTIVALS

SHOESTRING BUDGET

Only one pair of shoes was needed for an authentic Seattle vibe—anything more was extravagant. Eight-hole Dr. Martens were popular (or leather-free classic Converse or Vans for vegans).

Buy second-hand so they look worn-in

Knitted beanie is the grunge essential

Scruffy, straight hair

Dressing Down

Grunge started out as a music scene in Seattle in 1989, but the plaid shirts and beanies worn by the bands soon went mainstream.

Since grunge first became popular, it has kept creeping back into fashion. This makes perfect sense for three reasons. One: casual clothing is comfortable. Two: layering gives you a flexible wardrobe. Three: It's super cheap, because most of it can be picked up secondhand. Marc Jacobs first put grunge on the catwalk and made it high fashion, and he also mixed grunge elements, such as plaid, into later collections. Where Marc goes, others are sure to follow.

Layer T-shirts, jackets, and thrift-shop finds

Plaid shirt tied at waist

Combat boots (chunky socks optional)

Get the Look

♥ TATTOO NECKLACE: Tribal tattoos (in fact, any tattoos) were a big part of the Seattle scene. Fake it with a stretchy tattoo necklace.

♥ CUTOFF DENIM SHORTS in distressed denim—wear over a pair of tights in winter, or with bare legs and combat boots in summer.

| Black | Maroon | Brown | Mustard | Army green |

♥ FLANNEL SHIRT inspired by the buttoned-up shirts worn by lumberjacks felling trees in the forests of America. Wear yours open or tied around the waist—or one of each, for the real grunge version.

Urban **Clash**

In the 1990s fashion had a personality crisis. As well as grunge, there was preppy (the back-to-school look), vintage boho, lean and body-conscious (perfect for supermodels), and sporty-casual.

Florals and plaid together, you don't care

Runway grunge (low maintenance, high price)

BLACK AND WHITE
If you bought only one thing in the 1990s, it had to be black and white, cropped, and tight.

CASUAL GLAMOUR
A backpack said you were laidback, but one in leather meant you were more chic than sporty.

FROM GRUNGE TO IVY LEAGUE
Preppy girls loved plaid miniskirts (but wouldn't be seen dead in a grungy plaid shirt).

LV FOREVER
Grunge girls carried a thrift shop shoulder bag, while everyone else lusted after a Louis Vuitton tote.

DESIGNER OF THE DECADE
Gianni Versace was the darling of the 1990s, designing body-skimming dresses that were feminine and fierce.

> Do you prefer 'fashion victim' or 'ensembly challenged'?

Cher Horowitz in the movie *Clueless*

Looks like your top is tucked into your jeans

Stretch satin fabric + Hand-painted flowers = Body-con fantasy for late '90s

BODYSUIT CRAZE
The "body" was the most uncomfortable item of the decade—with snap fasteners "down under."

THE SPICE GIRLS' FIRST SINGLE WENT TO NO. 1 WORLDWIDE IN 1996, AND SO DID THEIR FASHION INFLUENCE—FROM "SPORTY" IN SNEAKERS TO "POSH" IN STILETTOS, AND THE OTHER THREE IN HUGE PLATFORMS.

SNEAKER CHIC
Designer Donna Karan picked up on the casual streetwear vibe and started making sports-inspired fashion.

Good-bye to dressing down; hello to romance

MOST MEMORABLE MOMENT
In 1993, supermodel Naomi Campbell toppled over on the catwalk in Vivienne Westwood's 10-inch (25-cm) platforms.

BODY BEAUTIFUL
Supermodels loved Dolce & Gabbana so much they offered to walk in the shows in exchange for clothes.

The **Front** Row

The runway is fabulous but the real show happens in the first three rows—the only ones that count! There's a rush for the goody bags and a nightmare "twin moment" when two celebs wear the same outfit. Who gets a front-row, or *frow*, seat and who gets bumped to the back?

THE BLOGGER
Last year row 7; this year, thanks to 2 million followers, she's made the fourth row, and got the backstage pass to interview the designer.

THE MODEL
Up since 2am for fittings. One minute to walk the runway; three minutes to change into next outfit. Walks tall in heels two sizes too small.

THE SOCIALITE
This uptown girl buys up big each season. The designer calls her his "muse" and often thinks of her when planning collections.

THE SHOW PRODUCER
On a big budget! Soft pink lighting to flatter the celebs + venue rental + hair and makeup + models + etc adds up to $150 a second for a 10-minute show.

THE EDITOR
Gets the best seat to view the outfits, two-thirds along the runway. Limo outside so she doesn't have to go far in her killer heels.

THE CELEBRITY
Flown in first-class so that he can take his pick of the collection, but so worth it. What he's wearing now will sell out because of photos of him at the show.

"It's all about the **audience**."
Karl Lagerfeld, designer

ANOTHER EDITOR
Her magazine is not as popular as it used to be, and she gave the designer a so-so review for the last collection, so her seat is further back.

THE GOODY BAG
The editor leaves her goody bag for her assistant in the row behind, who has already grabbed extras to sell online.

THE PHOTOGRAPHER
Camera linked so photos go straight to magazines, newspapers, and websites. Front row pics already up— frowers dressed up for him.

THE POWER BUYER
Major department store buyer; she can make or break a designer. Looking for good basics, fun accessories, and cool dresses for the window.

THE COMPETITION
She sneakily takes photos of catwalk designs on her phone, or watches them streamed online. In 5 weeks, copies will be in store.

THE RIVAL EDITOR
Once fashion director for "The Editor" but now works for a rival. The two are always seated far apart.

A day in the life of a

RUNWAY **MODEL**

At 19 years old, French model Marine Deleeuw lives a life many girls dream about. But modeling isn't just about big paychecks and free clothes; it's about early starts and late nights, and very little time to call your own.

Marine Deleeuw
Top Model

6AM

Marine makes her bed in the Paris flat she shares with several models from the agency.

9AM

Her manager has set a casting for later that morning. Marine takes a car across town to the studio.

1PM

Every model arrives backstage with a clean, bare face so the makeup artist can start work.

2PM

It takes an hour to get Marine's hair into a braided bun with a dead-straight center part.

3PM

Marine tries on the designer's strappy gold sandals. The heels are high but she's used to that.

> "On days when I do not work, I am **working on my image**. I have to hit the gym. I have **beauty appointments**. I have to **work toward my next job** and maintaining my image, **just like an athlete**."
>
> Linda Evangelista, top model, 2012

10AM

Designer Zuhair Murad is casting for a show. Marine puts on one of his dresses and waits to be seen.

11AM

She's perfect! Zahair makes a few last-minute adjustments to the dress for the final fitting.

12PM

There's often a three-hour wait before a show starts. Marine gets some fresh air and calls home.

Every detail is perfect for the start of the show, but there are several quick changes to come.

4PM

The atmosphere is electric, but the famous faces at the front are a blur. Marine just walks!

6PM

The show's over and Marine heads to the airport for her flight to New York for Fashion Week.

Being
Kate

She started out as a schoolgirl with bowed legs, a flat chest, crooked teeth, and scruffy hair, yet Kate Moss has become a global fashion phenomenon.

Her rocker-chick fashion combinations are copied by girls around the world, and her design collaborations with chain stores and luxury brands have been sellouts. But what is Kate's secret? She never looks too perfect or polished, and she never wears a whole fashion look from head to toe. As a teenager she couldn't afford to, so she learned how to put outfits together with items hunted down at secondhand shops.

Kate was spotted by a model agent at JFK airport when she was just 14. She famously posed for legendary fashion photographer Corinne Day, looking like a normal teenager on a Saturday morning, with a sweet smile and messy hair, appearing makeup free and completely unstyled. She was natural and a little bit grungy—the complete opposite of the Amazonian supermodels of the early 1990s.

Winter shades for daytime cool

Statement coat dressed down with hands in pockets

Skinny rock 'n' roll jeans with everything

Slouchy, Western-style ankle boots

SUPER STYLING
A natural parting and loose, slightly messy locks (teased with a brush) give Kate the perfect bedhead look. Minimal makeup adds to the illusion that she isn't trying, but Kate likes a feline eye created with eyeliner along the lash line, softened with a brush.

CLASSIC KATE
Kate's love of skinny jeans has helped to keep the trend alive for the past 10 years.

FESTIVAL CHIC
Kate first wore the vest, shorts, and Hunter boots combo to Glastonbury, UK, in 2005 and it became one of her most copied looks.

Men's wear classic style, shaped for feminine figure

Little tailored shorts or denim cutoffs

Delicate jeweled accessories add individuality

WINDOW DRESSING
When Kate posed in a Topshop window to promote her new collection, she chose a favorite style—a 1930s-inspired dress.

Vintage-inspired dress in an unexpected color

Walk with confidence, in flats or heels

Hunters are a music festival essential, even if it's not raining

The Wish List

★ LEOPARD PRINT: Animal print has been in fashion since it became popular in the 1950s; follow Kate's modern take and pair a leopard print coat, scarf, shoes, or bag with black basics.

★ VINTAGE DRESS: Kate's secondhand clothes are often vintage designer pieces, but search thrift shops and markets for cheaper options.

★ CLASSIC BLACK TOTE: A roomy, semi-structured bag with handles (and optional shoulder strap) is a Kate Moss essential.

★ DELICATE JEWELS: Kate piles on lots of tiny gold rings so she never looks too formal.

Modern **Dressing**

Today women have four times as many clothes as they did in the 1980s, and we just can't stop shopping. The average number of items bought in one year has risen rapidly from 50 in 1992 to more than 100 today, but do we look more stylish as a result?

When the sewing machine was invented, back in the mid-1800s, clothing became quicker to make—an hour of hand stitching was replaced by 10–15 minutes of machine stitching. So clothes became cheaper and women were tempted to buy more of them. Today, we can afford more clothes than ever because of cheap manufacturing, especially in Asia, which means low prices in stores. But since news reports about unsafe working conditions and child labor, people have started to think more about where their clothes come from and who makes them, and question whether cheap necessarily equals good and "must-have."

★ WE WEAR 20 PERCENT of our wardrobe 80 percent of the time.

★ FASHION DESIGNERS used to make two collections a year— summer and winter. Now they design up to 18 collections a year.

★ IN THE 1950s fashion magazines advised young working women to buy their wardrobes on a 3-year plan, buying one major item a year, like a coat, and spending the rest of their clothing allowance on smaller, cheaper things.

★ TODAY'S HOMES have three times as much closet space as those in the 1950s.

★ AS MANY AS 22 items hanging in a woman's closet have never been worn, tags still attached.

★ ENVIRONMENTAL GROUPS are getting worried about how much energy is used in making and shipping clothes, and how much discarded stuff ends up in landfills.

★ WOMEN HAVE THREE TIMES as many clothes as men.

★ PEOPLE IN SWEDEN buy more new clothes each year than those in almost any other country.

★ DONATION BINS in clothing stores or parking lots offer an alternative to throwing away unwanted clothes.

★ 80 BILLION PIECES of clothing are made each year.

TEN A SEASON

If you want fewer clothes, try the ten-item capsule wardrobe; French women swear by it. You need just ten main items in summer and ten in winter. From these core pieces you can mix and match to create more than 30 outfits.

YOUR TEN ESSENTIALS

② PAIRS OF JEANS, or one pair of jeans and one pair of nice pants

① SKIRT or pair of shorts

④ TOPS that go with the bottoms (remember the color scheme!)

① CARDIGAN or sweater

① LIGHT JACKET

① DRESS

Choose a color scheme, like gray, white, and blue, and start to mix and match

Shoes, accessories, and coats are extra.

Global **Runway**

For more than 300 years Paris reigned as the fashion capital of the world, but today its fashion shows have many rivals. From New York to Sydney, cities around the world are hosting their own fashion weeks that showcase local designs.

PARIS, FRANCE:
Feb/Mar and Sept/Oct
The world has been following Paris trends since the 1670s, when French publishers launched the first fashion magazines. The first fashion show was presented there, too, by celebrity couturier Charles Frederick Worth, and since then Paris has kept its reputation for innovative and elegant designs.

MILAN, ITALY: Feb/Mar and Sept/Oct
Launched in 1951 in Florence, Italian Fashion Week was so successful that there wasn't a venue big enough in the city to continue hosting it, so the event moved to Milan in 1958. Italian fashion is renowned for glamour, luxurious fabrics, and fine tailoring.

LONDON, UK: Feb/Mar and Sept/Oct
London Fashion Week began in 1984 in a west London parking lot, and has helped launch the careers of many, including Alexander McQueen, Stella McCartney, and Kate Moss. It established itself alongside Paris, Milan, and New York, and is now considered to be the best place for edgy, street-inspired designs.

NEW YORK, US:
Feb and Sept
New York's Fashion Week was launched in 1943 to give the industry a boost—during World War II, American buyers and journalists couldn't travel to Paris. The city is best known for producing pared-down separates and sportswear.

SAO PAOLO, BRAZIL: Mar and Oct
Supermodel Gisele Bündchen launched her career at the age of 14 in Sao Paolo. It's the place to see colorful clothes, leather work, modern jewelry, and designs that reveal lots of skin.

STOCKHOLM, SWEDEN: Jan/Feb and Aug
While fashion editors and buyers wait for the main fashion shows in New York, London, Milan, and Paris, they flock to Scandinavia's style capital for high-quality, minimalist fashion that is very affordable.

MOSCOW, RUSSIA: Mar and Oct
Although Russians are among the biggest fashion spenders in the world, their local designers are almost unknown. But the opulence and rich fabrics of Russian clothing inspired many designers in the 1920s, as well as Yves Saint Laurent in the 1970s, and recent collections by Louis Vuitton and Chanel.

ISTANBUL, TURKEY: Mar and Oct
Living on the edge of Europe and Asia, Turkish fashion designers create clothes for fashionistas—followers of Western fashion—and "hijabistas"—the word used for chic Islamic women who wear the traditional hijab head-scarf.

BEIJING, CHINA: Mar and Oct
Young Chinese are obsessed with luxury overseas brands, but local fashion designers do shows at China Fashion Week twice a year. There is a new breed of creative young designers emerging who are expected to be a strong force in international fashion.

MUMBAI, INDIA: Feb and Aug
Fashion in India is all about dressing for special events like weddings and festivals. Customers love surface decoration, so designers specialize in very glitzy outfits, often inspired by Bollywood costumes, and incorporating elements of traditional clothing, like the sari.

SYDNEY, AUSTRALIA: April
Once the place for buyers seeking the world's best swim wear, Sydney now attracts fashion editors and buyers with its upcoming young designers, too. For bloggers it's the place to capture sunny street style.

TOKYO, JAPAN: Mar and Oct
Japanese designers have a reputation for creating quirky, highly artistic clothes, like those produced by famous labels Comme des Garcons and Yohji Yamamoto, who show in Paris. Japanese fashion is especially loved in other parts of Asia, such as Hong Kong and Taiwan.

What **Next?**

Fast-forward just a few years and the way we dress might be very different—from print-your-own 3-D shoes, to jewelry that lets your friends know where you are. In fact, some of these surprising creations are ready to wear now.

Chip tracks your location

WHERE AM I?
This bracelet by CuffLinc communicates like a cell phone—just tap to send a message.

HIGH-ENERGY STYLE
You can walk, swim, or sleep while wearing this Misfit Shine sensor, which monitors your activity.

DESIGNERS ARE DEVELOPING BUTTONS THAT WILL CHANGE THE COLOR OF YOUR CLOTHES WHEN PUSHED

TRACK PERFORMANCE
Measure your fitness, and look fashionable at the same time, with an intelligent wristband.

AM I BLUSHING?
Share your feelings with the world by wearing clothes that change color with your mood (made by futuristic fabric-maker Sensoree).

SHINING STAR
Bring dazzle to red carpet occasions like Katy Perry, wearing a dress that literally lights up.

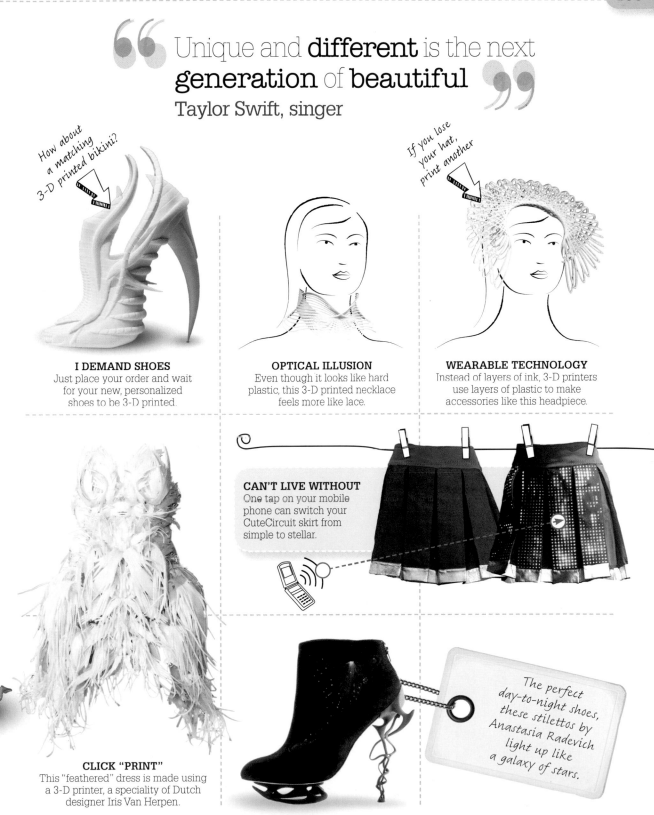

" Unique and **different** is the next **generation** of **beautiful** "

Taylor Swift, singer

How about a matching 3-D printed bikini?

If you lose your hat, print another

I DEMAND SHOES
Just place your order and wait for your new, personalized shoes to be 3-D printed.

OPTICAL ILLUSION
Even though it looks like hard plastic, this 3-D printed necklace feels more like lace.

WEARABLE TECHNOLOGY
Instead of layers of ink, 3-D printers use layers of plastic to make accessories like this headpiece.

CAN'T LIVE WITHOUT
One tap on your mobile phone can switch your CuteCircuit skirt from simple to stellar.

CLICK "PRINT"
This "feathered" dress is made using a 3-D printer, a speciality of Dutch designer Iris Van Herpen.

The perfect day-to-night shoes, these stilettos by Anastasia Radevich light up like a galaxy of stars.

"And now, I'm just trying to **change the world,** one sequin at a time."
Lady Gaga SINGER

"**Clothes** aren't going to **change** the world, the **women** who wear them will."
Anne Klein DESIGNER

"To me, fashion is like a mirror. **It's a reflection** of the times."
Anna Sui DESIGNER

"Fashion is instant **language**."
Miuccia Prada DESIGNER

"Style is a way to say **who you are** without having to speak."
Rachel Zoe STYLIST

"**Fashion** is in the sky, in the street. Fashion has to do with **ideas,** the way we live, **what is happening.**"
Coco Chanel DESIGNER

"Create your own style… **let it be unique for yourself** and yet identifiable for others."
Anna Wintour EDITOR, VOGUE

"The fashionable woman wears clothes. The clothes don't wear her."
Mary Quant DESIGNER

"I have **too many clothes,** I have too many options."
Rhianna SINGER

"**Fashion** should be a form of **escapism**."
Alexander McQueen DESIGNER

"When in doubt **wear red**."
Bill Blass DESIGNER

"**Simplicity**, good taste, and **grooming** are the three **fundamentals** of good **dressing**."
Christian Dior DESIGNER

"One is never overdressed or underdressed with a **Little Black Dress**."
Karl Lagerfeld DESIGNER

"Fashions fade, **style is eternal**."
Yves Saint Laurent DESIGNER

"There's nothing interesting about looking perfect... You want what you're wearing to say **something about you,** about who you are."
Emma Watson ACTOR

"Fashion draws **inspiration from** the best of **the past**."
Lana Del Rey SINGER

Illustrated Glossary

A

A-LINE A triangular dress shape with the skirt or dress flaring out like the sides of the letter "A." Christian Dior first used the phrase, calling his 1955 collection "A-line."

ACCESSORY Any item that is worn to complete an outfit, such as shoes, jewelry, bags, gloves, and hats. In the last 30 years, accessories have become more important to the fashion business than clothing itself.

APRON A piece of fabric or leather that is tied around the body to protect clothing, especially for cooking, housework, or manual work.

ARMLET Metal or leather band that is worn around the upper arm (above the elbow). Popular as jewelry for both men and women in Ancient Greece.

ART DECO An art movement of the 1920s that was picked up by fashion designers, interior designers, and architects. The look was simple, sleek, and geometric, and was inspired by new types of machines such as factory-made cars and airplanes.

ART NOUVEAU A style of European art that appeared in the late 1800s, based on the organic curves and swirls of nature. It influenced architecture, interior design, and fashion.

AVIATOR SUNGLASSES Wire-framed sunglasses made by Ray-Ban in 1936 to protect pilots' eyes from sun glare (which was known to cause headaches and altitude sickness). The original models had green lenses.

B

BABOUCHES Slipper traditionally worn by Arab desert tribes, especially the Bedouin. They are typically made from leather and are either backless or the heel is folded down so they can be slipped on.

BACKPACK A sacklike bag worn on your back, with straps over the shoulders. The oldest backpack in the world is 5,000 years old, found on a mummified man in the Italian Alps. It was made from goatskin, stretched around a wooden frame.

BALL GOWN A long dress made from luxurious fabric, usually with a fitted top and full skirt, worn to a formal dance, or ball. In the 1800s, balls were a place for meeting a potential husband so the ball gown was an important fashion item.

BALLERINA SKIRT A full, bell-shaped skirt finishing just above the ankle. The first ballerina skirts were the long tutus of frothy white tulle made for the dancers in the 1832 ballet *La Sylphide*.

BALLERINA WRAP Cropped, slim-fit, V-neck cardigan that crosses over at the front and ties around the body— usually made of stretch jersey and traditionally worn by dancers while they warm up.

BALLET FLATS Light shoes with a flat heel, made from thin leather or fabric. Designed like the dance shoes worn by ballerinas but with a thicker sole and heel

to make them suitable for wearing outside.

BANDANA A handkerchief folded into a triangle and worn tied around the neck or head; it traditionally has a white pattern on either a red or blue background.

BANGLE A stiff circular or oval-shaped band that can be slipped over the hand and worn as a piece of jewelry on the wrist. A bangle is usually made of metal, such as silver or gold, but it can also be made of wood or plastic.

BASE A piece of basic clothing that is the starting point for putting an outfit together. It could be jeans or black pants, or a black skirt, or a simple white T-shirt.

BELL-BOTTOMS Style of pants that fit close around the hips but with legs that flare out to become very wide at the bottom. First worn by sailors as part of their naval uniform, but became fashionable in the 1970s.

BERET A soft, circular cap made from wool or felt, sometimes worn tilted on the side. Part of the traditional outfit worn by people in the Basque region of France and Spain.

BIKINI Two-piece bathing suit for women. It was invented in 1946 by a Frenchman named Louis Réard, who ran his mother's underwear business in Paris.

BLOOMERS Baggy knickerbockers worn by women for cycling and other sports in the mid 1800s; also loose, knee-length women's underpants. At the time, it was shocking for a woman to wear bloomers, and they were banned from some public places.

BLOUSE A light, soft shirt for women, usually in cotton, linen, or silk. The blouse was first worn by working men in the 1800s because it was loose and comfortable and could be easily washed.

BOA A long scarf made of feathers or fur. It is named after the boa constrictor snake, which wraps tightly around its prey.

BOATER Stiff straw hat that is flat on top with a straight brim. Traditionally trimmed with a striped ribbon, it was popular in the late 1800s and early 1900s as a casual summer accessory for men and women.

BOBBY PIN A thin, double-ended wire hair pin that slides into the hair to hold it in place. Became very popular in the 1920s to hold short "bobbed" hair in place (which is how the pin got its name).

BOBBY-SOXER Teenage girls of the 1950s who wore ankle socks and flat shoes with their full skirts. The word "bobby" in "bobby-soxer" comes from the phrase "to bob," meaning to cut short, because their socks were short.

BODICE The upper part of a garment, especially a dress, between the shoulders and the waist.

BODYSUIT An all-in-one in the style of a leotard or a one-piece bathing suit, with snaps (press studs) at the crotch to enable the bodysuit to be undone. A bodysuit was designed to be worn under pants or a skirt, to create the appearance of a fitted T-shirt.

BOHO Short for bohemian, a clothing style that is arty, romantic, and exotic. It usually includes flowing, loose clothing, such as harem pants.

BOLERO A very short-cropped, decorative, open jacket for women, most often worn with a dress. It was inspired by traditional Spanish men's jackets.

BONNET In medieval times, a bonnet was a head covering made from soft fabric. However, by the 1700s it had become a shaped women's hat with a small brim only at the front, often tied under the chin with ribbons.

BOW TIE Formal necktie with a compact, symmetrical bow, originally worn as part of men's evening wear with white shirt and black tuxedo.

BOYFRIEND JEANS Slouchy jeans worn by women, meant to look as though they have been borrowed from a boyfriend. They sit low on the hips, are slightly baggy, and the bottoms are rolled up to show the ankles.

BOWLER A hard felt hat with a rounded top, the bowler was worn for horse riding in the 1800s, and later became a stylish hat for men.

BRAND The name and logo attached to a product. Fashion companies often own several brands, each one targeted at a different type of customer. The logo can be one of the most important parts of the brand; the most successful brands have logos that are instantly recognizable.

BRASSIÈRE (BRA) Women's underwear for supporting the bust. The word was first used to mean a bra in 1893, by an underwear company that thought it would sound more glamorous to use a French word for its new bust supporter (in French, "brassière" means a baby's vest top or undershirt).

BREECHES Men's fitted pants that finish at the knee. In the 1700s these were popular with men who paired them with stockings to cover the lower leg.

BROOCH A piece of jewelry that is pinned to clothing. In many ancient cultures brooches were used to hold clothing together, as well as for decoration.

BUSK A flat piece of whalebone, wood, or metal used to stiffen the front of a corset, or stays. Wooden busks were often hand-carved and decorated with hearts or initials.

BUSTIER An item of underwear or lingerie that combines a bra and a camisole. It reaches from the top of the bust to the waist and usually has boning in it to make the upper body more curvaceous.

BUSTLE A frame or padding worn under the back of a skirt, just below the waist, to hold up the fabric and stop it from dragging. Bustles were used to create the dress shape that was fashionable between the middle of the 1800s and the end of that century.

BUSTLE PAD A small pillow that is attached behind the wearer's waist, under her clothes, to make the skirt stick out from the body.

C

CAMISOLE Sleeveless top with thin straps that finishes around the waist. It is usually worn under clothing as underwear but can also be worn on its own.

CAPE Form of outerwear worn instead of a coat. Cut in a semicircle and attached at the neckline, it wraps around the body for warmth.

CAPRI PANTS Fitted women's pants that finish above the ankle. They were first worn in the 1950s as summer casual wear, and made especially popular by actress Audrey Hepburn.

CARDIGAN A knitted jacket fastened at the front by buttons or a zipper. First worn by soldiers in the Crimean War (1853–1856), by the 1920s it had become

casual wear for both men and women.

CATWALK Another word for "runway," a catwalk is the long, narrow walkway on which models show a designer's clothes. It's called a "cat" walk because you have to walk carefully, like a cat, so you don't fall off.

CHEMISE The original meaning is an undershirt made of linen or cotton that was worn by men and women for centuries. Now a chemise is a thigh-length strappy top worn under dresses (like a longer version of a camisole).

CHIC Pronounced "sheek" in English, it is a French word that means stylish or fashionable, but not trying too hard.

CHOKER A band or ribbon worn as jewelry around the throat. It is often decorated with a pendant or other type of small jewel.

CLOCHE A close-fitting women's hat with a slightly flared brim that creates a bell shape. It was fashionable during the 1920s, when it was usually worn over short hair.

COCKTAIL HAT Small, decorative hat worn for early evening cocktail parties. Unlike other hats, which are meant to be taken off indoors, a cocktail hat should stay on.

COLLAR Anything that can be worn around the neck, but usually the collar is attached to an article of clothing such as a shirt or dress.

CONE HAT A headdress in the shape of an upside-down ice-cream cone, also called a hennin. It was worn by European women in medieval times, and before that by Mongol warrior queens.

CORDUROY A cotton fabric with a soft, velvety surface and fine ridges or lines running down it. Typically used for outdoor jackets

and pants because it is warm and tough.

CORSAGE The bodice of a woman's dress; also a bunch of flowers pinned to a woman's bust or shoulder, or worn on the wrist.

CORSET Support underwear that looks like a sleeveless top but has stiff strips sewn into it so that it holds in the stomach to create a small waist. Since the late 1990s it has also been worn as outerwear.

COTTON Type of fabric woven from the fluffy fibers of the cotton plant. First used in Asia, but now worn by people around the world, especially in hot climates.

CRAVAT Cloth worn around the neck, especially by fashion-conscious men in

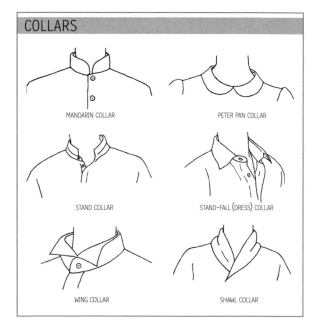

COLLARS

MANDARIN COLLAR

PETER PAN COLLAR

STAND COLLAR

STAND-FALL (DRESS) COLLAR

WING COLLAR

SHAWL COLLAR

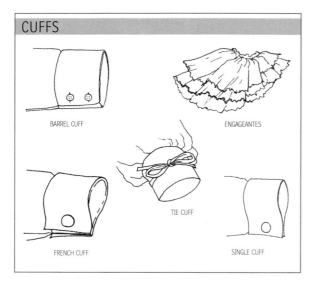

CUFFS

BARREL CUFF

ENGAGEANTES

TIE CUFF

FRENCH CUFF

SINGLE CUFF

1700s and 1800s. It came to Europe from Croatia, where it was part of men's traditional dress. It is still worn today as a dressy accessory, often in patterned silk.

CRINOLINE Also called a cage petticoat, a crinoline was dome shaped and worn under skirts as support. It was made from strips of whalebone or wire hoops and held with fabric tape. Crinoline fabric was made of horsehair and cotton.

CROP TOP A top that is cut short to show the midriff. It became fashionable during a fitness craze in the 1980s when women wanted to show off their toned bodies.

CUFF The section at the end of a sleeve, sometimes thicker than the rest of the sleeve. It can have buttons for fastening or can be designed to be worn turned back.

D

DANDY A man who takes great care in how he grooms himself and what he wears, dressing in a precise, gentlemanlike style. The "dandy" dates from the late 1700s, and Beau Brummel was the most famous dandy of that time.

DÉCOLLETAGE A low-cut neckline on a woman's dress.

DENIM Thick cotton fabric made with one colored thread and one white thread. Used since the 1600s to make practical work wear, as well as for upholstery and boat sails. Blue denim has been used for jeans since the late 1800s.

DESIGN COLLABORATION A team effort in which two designers work together to create a new product. For example, when a major brand

pays an up-and-coming designer to help create a fresh product.

DINNER JACKET A man's jacket for formal eveningwear, often with silk-faced or satin-faced lapels. It's commonly known as a tuxedo.

DRAWERS Type of undergarment worn in the 1500s and later. They were usually made from cotton or linen and were long, sometimes to the ankle.

DRESS CLOTHES Formal garments for men, particularly for evening, such as a tailcoat.

DUCKTAIL Hairstyle popular in the 1950s among fashion conscious males. Hair was greased, and each side combed back around the head to meet at the back (looking like a duck viewed from behind).

E

EMBROIDERY Decorative stitching on fabric, such as silk, wool, and cotton. Up until the late 1800s, most women made their own clothes, so learning how to embroider was a useful skill.

ESPADRILLES Canvas shoes with rope soles, which either slip on or are held on with ankle ties. They were

worn by French and Spanish peasants for centuries but are now popular summer footwear for men and women.

F

FARTHINGALE A very wide, stiff underskirt designed to support a gown and expand its shape. Worn from the mid 1500s until the 1620s, the farthingale was made from wicker, wire, or whalebone hoops.

FASCINATOR A cross between a little hat and a hair clip, the fascinator is a delicate head ornament usually made of feathers and net. (It's meant to make you look "fascinating.")

FAUX FUR Fake fur that is made from synthetic materials instead of animal fur. It is much cheaper than real fur and is popular among shoppers who don't want to wear the real thing for ethical reasons.

FELINE EYE Commonly referred to as a "cat eye." In makeup, this is a cat-shaped eye which looks turned up at the far corners. The look is usually created by applying eyeliner on the upper lids and sweeping it up beyond the outer edge of the eye.

FISHNET Mesh fabric made up of tiny diamond shapes (called "fishnet" because it looks like the open weave of a fishing net). Mostly used for women's stockings and tights.

FISHTAIL TRAIN
A cascading section of a dress or skirt that flares out from the knee down to the ground and beyond. The hem is longer at the back and trails on the ground.

FLAPPER A fashionable young woman of the 1920s who craved independence, fun times, and a modern image. Her look included short hair and knee-length dresses.

FLARES Pants that fit tightly around the waist and hips, and flare out from the knee down, becoming wide at the bottom. Another word for bell-bottoms.

FOB WATCH Also called a pocket watch, this is a watch (no wrist strap) attached to a short chain. The chain is pinned to clothing and the watch sits in a pocket—traditionally in the pocket of a man's waistcoat.

FOUNDATION GARMENT
Anything that's worn under clothing to control and smooth the shape of the body, such as full briefs made from high-stretch fabric. Also called shapewear.

FRINGING A band of decoration made up of many small threads or strips. Usually hangs off clothing at the hem or sleeve edges but can also be used to cover a whole dress or outfit.

FROGGING A way of doing up a coat or jacket instead of buttons, frogging is made from fancy knotted braid, or cord, with a loop made out of the braid on one side and a small button made from braid on the other side.

FROW An abbreviation for the front row—the row of seats closest to the runway of a fashion show. Reserved for the most important guests, such as celebrities and powerful magazine editors.

FUR The skin of an animal with the fur kept on. It can be made into a whole garment—such as a fur coat—used as a lining inside clothes, or used as a trim or accessory. Traditionally worn by indigenous tribes living in the Arctic.

G

GARTER An elasticated band that is slipped onto the leg and placed around the upper thigh to hold up stockings.

GIRDLE In medieval times, a girdle was a belt or cord worn around the waist to keep clothing in place. By the 1920s the girdle had become a thick elasticated band worn around the stomach and hips to create a smooth shape under clothes.

GO-GO BOOTS Knee-high boots for women, with a low or flat heel and often a chunky toe, inspired by "Space Age" style.

GOWN In medieval times, a gown was a long, loose garment worn by men and women. By the 1700s it was a long formal dress for women.

GRUNGE A messy or disheveled style of dressing down that usually includes thrift shop items and cheap outdoor wear. The look came from the grunge music scene that started in Seattle in the late 1980s.

H

HABIT Either the clothes traditionally worn by nuns and monks, or the dress once worn by women when riding horses (see *Riding Habit*).

HAREM PANTS Baggy pants made from soft fabric that are narrow around the ankles. They are part of the traditional dress in some countries, but became fashionable in Europe in the early 1900s.

HEADDRESS Anything wrapped around or covering the hair in a decorative way. A headdress can be worn for fashion (very popular in medieval and renaissance times), or for religious or cultural reasons.

HEAD-SCARF Square of fabric that is worn over the hair and tied in place. It is usually worn by women—to be fashionable, for practical reasons such as keeping the hair off the face, or to hide the hair because of religious beliefs.

HEELS The abbreviated way of saying "high-heeled shoes." Can also be paired with "killer," as in "killer heels," meaning shoes (usually stilettos) that are at least 4 inches (10 cm) high.

JACKETS

BLAZER

DINNER JACKET

DONKEY JACKET

DOUBLE-BREASTED

HACKING JACKET

MANDARIN JACKET

NEHRU JACKET

NORFOLK JACKET

PEA JACKET

SAFARI JACKET

SINGLE-BREASTED

SMOKING JACKET

HEMLINE The bottom edge of a dress or skirt. Hemlines are often the most obvious thing to change in fashion, going up or down every year, or every few years.

HIMATION A large rectangle of cloth that was worn in Ancient Greece by men and women. It could be draped, wrapped, and pinned in different ways, and was either worn on its own, or over other clothes.

HIPPIE Peace-loving style tribe of the late 1960s and early 1970s. Hippies tried to live a life in touch with nature, and wore handmade or recycled clothing, tie-dye patterns, and bright colors.

HORSE HAIR Hair from the tail and mane of live horses, which is woven into fabric; in the 19th century it was commonly used for women's padded undergarments.

HOT PANTS Very short, tight shorts. They were launched onto the fashion scene in the mid-1960s by London-based designer Mary Quant.

HOURGLASS A body shape with a big chest, tiny waist, and big hips (named after an old-fashioned hourglass or sandglass used to measure time). The hourglass figure has gone in and out of fashion, with corsets, belts, padding, or stretch fabrics used to create the effect.

HOUSE DRESS A casual and practical type of dress worn around the house for doing chores. Popular in the late 1800s and up until the end of the 1950s, it was an important item in the housewife's wardrobe.

J

JACKET A short coat for casual or outdoor wear. It usually finishes at the hips or waist, and is not as warm as a coat.

JADE A semiprecious stone, popular for jewelry. It can come in many colors but the most popular and valuable is bright green. It has special significance in China and North and South Korea as a symbol of power.

JEANS Tough pants made of denim, first worn by farm workers and others doing hard physical work, then made popular by cowboys in the movies. Since the 1950s, jeans have been common casual wear.

K

KIMONO A long Japanese robe made of cotton or silk, with very wide sleeves. It wraps across the body and is fastened with a wide fabric belt called an obi, which ties around the waist.

KIRTLE A long, fitted dress worn over a chemise (a light dress worn as an underlayer). It was laced up the front, back, or sides, so you could adjust the tightness of the fit.

KITTEN HEEL A women's shoe style that was launched in the late 1950s and is still popular in the 21st century.

It has a low stiletto heel that tapers to a tiny point.

L

LACE A delicate, decorated fabric with a pattern that resembles a spider's web. It used to be made by hand using cotton or silk thread, and was very expensive, but by the middle of the 1800s cheaper, machine-made lace had become available.

LAMPSHADE SHAPE Dress silhouette shaped like a table lamp, with a top half that flares out over a slim bottom half. Said to have been invented by French designer Paul Poiret around 1913.

LBD This is short for "Little Black Dress." Since Chanel made the short black dress fashionable in the 1920s, an LBD has become the most useful item in a woman's wardrobe (after jeans), according to fashion editors.

LEATHER Animal skin (called hide) that has been given a special treatment (called tanning) to make it smooth and supple, ready to be made into clothes, shoes, and bags.

LEG WARMER Woollen tube worn over the lower calves and ankles. Originally worn by ballet dancers to keep their muscles warm, leg warmers entered fashion in the 1980s, when dancewear

items became part of everyday wardrobes.

LEGGINGS Thick footless tights, cut off at the ankles or higher. Once worn mainly by dancers, leggings became fashionable in the 1980s under big T-shirts or mini skirts. Leggings in fashion date back to at least the 13th century.

LINEN A strong but lightweight fabric made by weaving the stems of flax plants. It is one of the oldest fabrics in the world and for centuries was used especially for underwear.

LOCKET A small metal charm, usually in the shape of a heart, oval, or circle, worn on a chain around the neck. It opens and closes, with a space inside for a photo or a lock of hair.

LOGO A symbol that is designed to be used in place of a full brand name. A logo is usually just letters or a word but sometimes an image, or a combination of both.

LOGO MANIA An obsession for owning fashion products with logos. The phrase refers especially to the 1990s when there was a craze for handbags with designer logos clearly visible.

LUCITE A type of clear, very strong plastic, invented in the 1930s and first used for aircraft windshields. Since the 1940s it has been used

for fashion accessories, including shoes, handbags, and jewelry.

M

MANTUA A women's gown that was in fashion for about a hundred years, from the mid 1700s to the mid 1800s. Its main feature was an overskirt that was pulled back on either side to show the petticoat underneath.

MARY JANE A flat shoe with a round toe and a strap that buckles over the ankle. They were first designed as children's shoes, but from the early 1920s the style was worn by women as well, usually with a high heel.

MAXI A full-length skirt that covers most of your legs. Long skirts had been worn by women for hundreds of years, but they were only called maxi skirts after the invention of the miniskirt in the 1960s.

MIDI A skirt that finishes around the mid calf. It was called a midi in the 1970s to

make it stand out from the miniskirt or maxi skirt, although mid-calf skirts had also been worn in the 1950s.

MILLINERY The art of making hats, which are often custom-made to fit a customer's head, and can be designed using different types of materials and trims.

MINI An abbreviation for "miniskirt" (see below).

MINISKIRT A short skirt with a hemline that finishes around the middle of the thigh. Caused a huge shock when it was first worn in the 1960s but quickly became a normal part of fashion.

MORNING DRESS A semiformal suit (usually gray) worn by men for daytime occasions, or a dress worn in the 1800s by wealthy women for having breakfast and lounging at home.

MUFF A small cylinder, or tube, often made of fur, with space inside for you to place your hands and keep them warm. Muffs were often worn instead of gloves in winter time, and were extremely fashionable for women in the 1700s and 1800s.

MULES Slip-on shoes with a heel that can be anywhere from very low to very high. The front of the shoe is usually completely covered. They were worn by men and women from the 1500s onward, but are now mainly worn by women.

MUSLIN A fine, light, semitransparent fabric made from cotton or linen. This material was popular for women's dresses in the late 1700s, but was so flimsy that a coat or warm shawl was usually needed on top.

NYLON The brand name for a family of artificial fibers (made from chemicals rather than natural ingredients). Invented in 1935, nylon soon became used for making tights and stockings because it was cheap, strong, and could be made to look sheer.

OVERALLS An all-in-one top and pants outfit. Up until the 1940s they were worn mainly by men for factory work to protect their clothes, but when women started factory work during World War II they also wore overalls.

OXFORDS Flat, lace-up leather shoes, with hidden eyelets for lacing so you can only see tiny holes from the top. They first became popular among students at Oxford University in the early 1800s.

Oxfords became fashionable for women in the 1920s.

P

PAGODA SLEEVE Elbow-length, bell-shaped sleeves on dresses that were in fashion between 1849 and the 1860s. They usually had ruffles attached at the bottom edge, which could be removed for washing.

PALETTE A selection of colors chosen by an artist for a particular artwork, or by a fashion designer for a specific collection.

PANELS Sections of material that are stitched together to create a garment. The stitching lines are called seams. Panels can be used to shape a piece of clothing—for example, to emphasize the waist or create a full skirt.

PANNIERS Also called side hoops, these were pads or frames attached to the hips and worn as underclothes to hold a skirt out at the sides. They were worn in the early 1700s but then fell out of fashion.

PANTALOONS Loose-fitting pants that were cropped above the ankles or higher, and worn as underwear in the late 1800s. Usually made from cotton so they could be easily washed.

PANTS An item of clothing that covers both legs from the waist to the ankles, with openings for each leg. Pants have been worn for centuries, especially by men, but started being worn by women in the early 1900s.

PANTYHOSE A leg covering similar to tights, joined at the top and in stretchy fabric but much sheerer than tights. Launched in the 1960s, pantyhose became immediately popular as they were ideal for wearing with miniskirts.

PAPARAZZI Photographers who follow celebrities during their everyday routines and snap them on the street,

hoping to sell the photos to magazines and newspapers. From the Italian word *paparazzo*, meaning an annoying buzzing sound.

PARASOL A sun umbrella, usually smaller than a rain umbrella and made from lighter fabric, even paper. Parasols were popular during the 1700s and 1800s when women wanted to have skin that was unblemished by the sun.

PARURE A set of matching jewelry, often featuring precious gems such as diamonds or rubies. The parure might include a necklace, earrings, bracelet, and tiara.

PANTS — BELL-BOTTOMS, BOOT-CUT PANTS, CAPRI PANTS, CIGARETTE PANTS, DRAINPIPE PANTS, PALAZZO PANTS

PLEATS

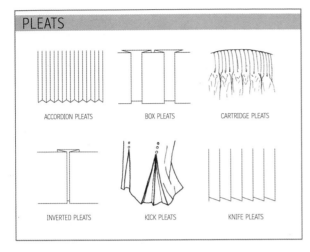

ACCORDION PLEATS   BOX PLEATS   CARTRIDGE PLEATS

INVERTED PLEATS   KICK PLEATS   KNIFE PLEATS

PATENT LEATHER A very shiny type of leather. The leather is coated with lacquer to give it a glossy look, and can be used for shoes, bags, belts, and items of clothing such as jackets.

PATTENS Overshoes that were worn over the top of regular shoes in order to protect them from rain and dirt. Pattens looked a lot like clogs and often had high wooden soles to lift the shoe above the dirt on the street.

PENDANT A small piece of jewelry that usually hangs from a chain necklace. Typical pendants include a locket made from silver or gold, a gemstone, a religious symbol such as a cross, or other decorative designs.

PEPLOS A type of garment worn by women in Ancient Greece; it was made from a large rectangle of fabric that was folded around the body and held in place with brooches and a belt.

PETTICOAT An underskirt worn by women. In past centuries the petticoat often included a frame of some kind that held out the skirt or dress worn over the top.

PIXIE CUT A short haircut with wisps of hair coming onto the face. Called a pixie cut because the look is like that of the imaginary pixie, a childlike magical creature that is part of ancient folk culture in many parts of Europe.

PLAID A woollen fabric, usually woven with a tartan or checked pattern. It is traditionally made into kilts and scarves and worn as part of the national clothing of Scotland. Plaid also became popular for workwear shirts and jackets because of its warmth.

PLATFORMS Shoes with a high heel and a very thick sole that can be almost as high as the heel. Platforms

have been worn throughout history, and were especially popular in the 1970s, when they were often teamed with bell-bottom pants.

PLEAT A narrow fold made in fabric by doubling it over and stitching it on one or both sides. Especially used for skirts, there are several different types of pleats, including hidden ones that are only visible when the wearer moves.

POCKET A section of fabric like a little bag or envelope that is incorporated into clothing to hold small objects. Women once used pockets to carry their valuables. These kinds of pockets weren't stitched into clothing; instead, they were worn like a pouch tied around the waist.

POLKA DOTS Pattern of filled-in circles spaced

evenly apart. The pattern started becoming popular in the 1880s at the same time as a dance called the polka. Polka dancers wore spotted jackets to show which dance club they were from and the fashion spread from there.

POP ART Art movement of the mid-1950s that turned everyday or popular images such as ads and cartoons into the subject of paintings and sculpture. For example, American artist Andy Warhol created artwork made from Campbell soup tin labels—a print that later inspired a minidress.

POUF Hairstyle in which hair was piled up over a wire frame or padding to create a tall egg shape, then lavishly decorated. Really fashionable around the middle of the 1700s, Marie Antoinette helped popularize it.

POCKETS

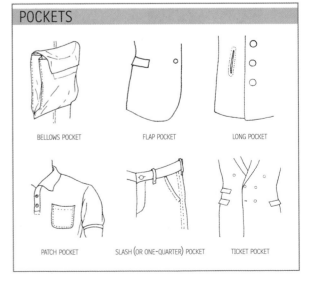

BELLOWS POCKET   FLAP POCKET   LONG POCKET

PATCH POCKET   SLASH (OR ONE-QUARTER) POCKET   TICKET POCKET

PREPPY A classic fashion style that gives the look of being a wealthy prep-school student. Key items are chinos and blazers, pleated skirts, and sweaters with a diamond pattern (called Fair Isle). Loafers are the essential footwear.

PROM DRESS Formal dress worn to a high school dance, usually held toward the end of the senior year of school. Proms were first held in the 1800s at colleges in the US but became really popular in the 1950s.

PROPORTIONS The size of each part of the body, in relation to the rest. In fashion, the goal is to put together all the parts of an outfit on the body to achieve an overall look that is balanced.

PUMPS Flat, slip-on shoes with toes, heels, and sides of the foot covered. The soles are thin and the leather is soft, like ballet shoes. They are now mostly worn by women, but in past centuries they were worn just as much by men.

PUNK A style tribe that formed in the late 1970s as a challenge to the fashions and ideas of the time. Their way of dressing included ripped clothes with safety pins, skinny jeans (when most other people were wearing flares), and Dr. Martens boots.

PVC Stands for polyvinyl chloride, a chemical substance that is used to coat fabrics, giving them a very glossy finish. Used in fashion during the 1960s, especially for boots and coats.

PAJAMAS Top and loose pants in soft fabric, worn to bed. The pants usually have elastic or a drawstring at the waist to make them comfortable. Fashion pajamas are a more luxurious version of bedtime pajamas and are meant to be worn as evening wear.

R

RA-RA SKIRT A short, frilled skirt, worn by cheerleaders and briefly popular in the 1980s.

READY-TO-WEAR Clothing sold in standard sizes that could be worn off-the-rack instead of having to be custom-made.

RETRO A fashion that has been inspired by the style of a few decades earlier. For example, wearing 1950s-style clothes, hair, or makeup can be called retro.

RHINESTONE Also called a diamanté, a rhinestone is a small decoration that looks a bit like a diamond. It has been used for jewelry and on clothing since the 1700s, and can be made from rock crystal, glass, or plastic.

RIBBON A long, thin band of fabric used for tying hair back, or for attaching to clothes as decoration or for tying. Originally, ribbons were made from silk.

RIDING BOOTS Knee-high boots, typically made from leather, used for horse riding. They fit tightly around the calves and are worn over slim riding pants.

RIDING HABIT The traditional outfit worn by women for riding horses since the middle of the 1700s. It includes a fitted jacket, shirt, long skirt, and men's-style hat.

ROBE In women's fashion, a robe was a dress with the front left open to show an underskirt. A robe could also mean a formal garment worn by men over the top of their other clothes. It later came to mean a dressing gown.

RUFF A detachable collar which is heavily pleated and sometimes starched to make it very stiff. Usually made of linen or lace, the ruff was worn by wealthy men and women in the 1500s and 1600s.

RUFFLES Frills or flounces, often used on the edges of collars, cuffs, and shirt fronts. They were especially popular with men in the 1500s. Although these days ruffles are worn mostly by women, men's formal shirts sometimes still have them.

RUNWAY In fashion, the runway (also called a catwalk) is the narrow, raised walkway on which models walk and stand to show off a designer's collections.

S

S-SHAPE A popular fashion silhouette in the late 1800s and early 1900s. It was achieved by wearing a special corset which pushed back the hips so the chest was thrust forward, creating a shape like the letter "S."

SACK BACK The name of a dress style in the 1700s, also called a *robe à la française* (it came from France). It had pleats running from the shoulders down the back of the dress, and was longer at the back so the hem trailed along the ground.

SAILOR PANT Wide-legged pants that are high waisted and fitted around the waist and hips, often with buttons at the side. The fashion world borrowed the style from sailors' naval uniforms in the 1920s.

SANDAL Shoe with straps across the front, exposing the toes. They are the

SKIRTS

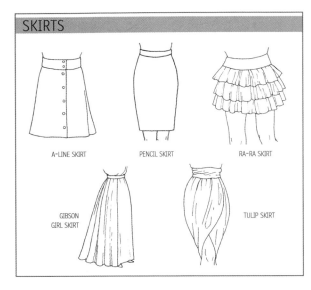

A-LINE SKIRT

PENCIL SKIRT

RA-RA SKIRT

GIBSON
GIRL SKIRT

TULIP SKIRT

earliest type of shoe, worn in many ancient cultures, especially in hot climates.

SATIN A fabric with a satin weave, a particular type of weaving technique that creates a smooth, shimmering effect on one side and a matte surface on the reverse.

SHAWL A rectangle or triangle of fabric that is worn draped around the back and over the shoulders and upper arms. The most famous shawls come from the province of Kashmir in India, where they have been worn for centuries.

SHIFT A word used until the 19th century to mean a woman's undershirt with long sleeves (looks kind of like a man's shirt); it was made of linen, but the poor used wool.

SHIFT DRESS A short, sleeveless dress (just a little bit longer than a mini dress) with a straight or slightly flared shape that skims the figure.

SILHOUETTE The outline of a shape, viewed from the side, straight on, or from behind. In fashion, the silhouette means the overall shape created by an outfit.

SILK Fine, luxurious fabric made from the cocoons spun by the caterpillars of silkworm moths. The technique for making silk was invented in China more than 2,000 years ago, and eventually came to Europe where people spent fortunes acquiring it.

SILK SATIN A type of silk that has a very smooth, shiny surface. The type of weaving used to create the glossy look is called a satin weave.

SKINNY JEANS Also called skinnies, they fit tightly to the body like a second skin and become narrower toward the ankle. They were launched in the 1950s but with a higher waist and not quite as tight at the ankles as modern skinnies.

SKIRT An item of clothing that fits around the waist and hangs down from there. Skirts are typically worn by women, but some types of skirts, such as kilts and sarongs, are also worn by men.

SLEEVE The part of a top, jacket, or dress that covers the arms. Sleeve shapes change with fashion and there are many different styles and lengths, from tiny, short cap sleeves to long, extra-wide kimono sleeves.

SLIDES A pair of slip-on shoes with straps over the front of the foot but nothing at the back so that

SLEEVES

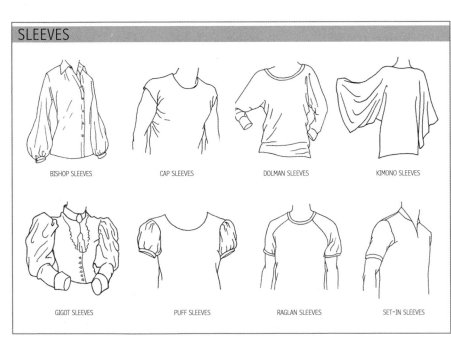

BISHOP SLEEVES

CAP SLEEVES

DOLMAN SLEEVES

KIMONO SLEEVES

GIGOT SLEEVES

PUFF SLEEVES

RAGLAN SLEEVES

SET-IN SLEEVES

they just slide on without the wearer having to bend down.

SLINGBACK Women's high-heeled shoe with either open or closed toes and a strap that goes around the back of the heel to hold the shoe on.

SLIP DRESS A dress that is shaped like a slip—a close-fitting, knee-length type of undergarment with thin straps, worn under dresses to create a smooth line. The slip dress is meant to be worn on its own.

SLIPPERS Light, low-heeled shoes that can easily be slipped on and off. Used for indoor wear, they were an important part of wealthy women's wardrobes in past centuries, since they spent so much time at home.

SNEAKERS Shoes worn for sports, with rubber, nonslip soles. The first sneakers were made from cotton canvas with simple rubber soles, and many sneaker styles are still made the same way.

STATUS BAG A luxury bag that everyone can recognize as being expensive, usually with a designer logo visible.

STAYS Like a corset, a stay was worn as underwear to give a fashionable shape under clothes. It fitted tightly around the bust and waist and was usually

stiffened with whalebone. It was heavier than a corset, and most women stopped wearing stays once corsets became popular in the 1800s.

STILETTO High, very thin heel on women's shoes. Invented in the 1950s, the stiletto heel is usually made with a metal spike inside to give it strength. The word *stiletto* means "knife" or "dagger" in Italian.

STOCKINGS Skintight leg coverings that are not joined at the top like pantyhose or tights. Each stocking in the pair is put on separately and held up with elastic around the upper thigh, or clipped onto a suspender belt.

STOLE A wide shawl or wrap, made of fur or luxurious fabric such as cashmere. It is worn around the shoulders and was especially popular in the 1800s for teaming with short-sleeved evening dresses.

STOMACHER A stiff, triangle-shaped panel, often beautifully embroidered, which was worn over the chest and stomach. In fashion from the 15th to the 18th centuries, it was worn under a dress that had an open section at the front so that the stomacher could be seen.

SUMPTUARY LAW Law that has been used since ancient times to tell people what

they can and cannot wear. There were many sumptuary laws between the 14th and 16th centuries, which tried to control how much money people were spending on luxury goods, and to stop the middle or lower classes from trying to look like they belonged to the upper class of society.

SUNDRESS Casual dress worn on hot summer days for keeping cool; it's usually sleeveless and made from cotton. Popular in the 1950s.

SUPERMODEL A fashion model who reaches celebrity status. A supermodel is recognized around the world and has the power to sell products just from his or her name, though most supermodels are women. The 1980s was the peak time for supermodels, who became very highly paid, earning millions of dollars for ad campaigns.

SURREALIST (SURREAL) An artist, writer, or designer who takes images and ideas from the imagination or dream world and places them in the real world in an unexpected way. This art style was big in the 1930s, and Salvador Dali was the most famous Surrealist of that time. Dali was one of several Surrealists to collaborate with fashion designer Elsa Schiaparelli on clothes and accessories, bringing the Surreal into fashion.

SUSPENDER BELT A soft, stretchy fabric band worn around the waist (under your clothes), with clips at the front and back for attaching stockings. Suspender belts were worn by almost all women in the 1940s and 1950s until pantyhose were invented in 1959.

SWEATER A loose-fitting, knitted, long-sleeved top that is pulled on over the head. It started as a garment worn by men in the late 1800s and by the first few decades of the 1900s it had become essential casual wear for both men and women.

T

T-SHIRT Simple top with sleeves made from cotton jersey. (It looks like a T-shape when laid on a flat surface). It has no buttons and slips on over the head. The T-shirt first became popular when worn by sailors as part of their naval uniform in the late 1800s.

T-STRAP SHOES Type of women's shoe, either flat or with heels, that has a center strap running along the top of the foot. The center strap joins to an ankle strap, making a "T" shape.

TAFFETA A type of silk with a crisp, paperlike texture and a shimmering surface.

There are also cheaper synthetic versions of taffeta. It is particularly used for evening wear styles that need a stiff type of fabric.

TANGO A style of dancing from Argentina in which the man and woman hold each other close (the dance takes its name from the Latin word *tango*, meaning "to touch"). It was extremely popular in Europe and America in the 1920s, and designers created clothes inspired by, and especially for dancing, the tango.

TEA GOWN Also called a tea dress, it is a long, loose, romantic style of dress worn by women in the UK in the late 1800s and early 1900s for having afternoon tea at home, or for visiting friends in the afternoon.

TEDDY GIRL The Teddy girls (and boys) were a style tribe in Britain in the 1950s. There were few nice clothes in the years straight after World War II, so they wore outfits inspired by the glamorous Edwardian era of the early 1900s (they abbreviated the word "Edwardian" to get "teddy"). Their style included little straw boaters, jackets with velvet collars, and pencil skirts.

THE BIG FOUR The four most important cities for showing designer fashion collections: New York City, London, Milan, and Paris. Twice a year, designers hold their fashion shows in one of these famous cities. There is a set schedule for the shows, which always start in New York City and finish in Paris.

THRIFT SHOP A store selling pre-owned clothes, also called secondhand clothes. Usually the clothes have been donated to the store, and a portion of the money received for each sale goes to charity.

TIE A strip of fabric (traditionally silk) that is worn under the collar of a shirt and knotted in a special way at the front. One section of the tie hangs down the front of the shirt and is meant to be part of an outfit. Mostly worn by men, but also by women since the late 1800s.

TOP HAT A men's hat style which is tall, flat on top, and with a small brim turned up at the sides. Worn for formal events, it is usually black and covered with fine, plush silk.

TOTE A roomy handbag for carrying, or "toting," things around. It usually has two handles, is open at the top, and is held in one hand.

TRAIN A long section at the back of a dress that trails along the ground. It has been a feature of women's fashion since medieval times, but these days is reserved for wedding dresses or red-carpet gowns.

TRICORN A hat with the brim turned up at the back and sides to form a triangle. It was first worn by soldiers and then became stylish in the 1700s. The tricorn was very practical in wet weather because the shape of the brim caught rainwater and drained it away at the back.

TUNIC A loose piece of clothing shaped like a long top, with sleeves or without, usually worn over a shirt and pants or leggings. It was an essential item in men's and women's wardrobes from ancient times until the medieval period.

TURBAN A headdress made by wrapping a long piece of cloth around the head; it was traditionally worn by men in parts of the Middle East and Asia. Turban-style hats (already formed and no need to wrap) have gone in and out of women's fashion since the 1800s.

TWO-TONE A combination of two different colors alongside each other, used especially for accessories— for example, two-tone shoes might be mostly black with a white section at the toe.

U

UNDERSKIRT A type of petticoat worn under a skirt or dress. It can either be stiffened to make the skirt on top stick out, or made of silky material to create a smooth surface and help the skirt hang smoothly.

UNDERSOLE The underneath section of the sole of a shoe (the part that touches the ground). It can also mean the under part of the foot.

UTILITY CLOTHING A collection of basic clothing produced by the government in Britain during World War II, since regular clothing factories had to put their efforts into making war uniforms and equipment.

V

VEIL A light, breathable fabric, partly see-through, that covers part of the hair and can be draped across the face. Worn mostly by women. Brides traditionally wear white veils.

VELOUR A smooth plush fabric made of cotton, wool, or synthetic fiber. It's similiar to velvet, but with a shorter pile.

VELVET A very luxurious silk fabric with a thick, soft surface that feels almost like fur. It was once extremely expensive but synthetic versions made from nylon and polyester are cheaper.

VELVETEEN An imitation velvet made from cotton, sometimes with a thin layer of silk on top. It started being made in the late 1700s to provide a cheaper version of velvet.

VEST Another name for a waistcoat (see right).

VICTORIAN GOTHIC A dramatic style of dressing in mostly black clothes made of velvet, lace, and leather. The look includes corsets (for women), black hair, and pale skin. It is inspired by fiction of the Victorian era (mid- to late-1800s), which mixed themes of romance and horror.

VICTORY ROLL A hairstyle worn by women during the years of World War II. The hair at the front and sides was swept off the face and into a roll above the forehead. Helped to keep women's hair from getting caught in machinery while they worked in factories.

VINTAGE Clothing and accessories from previous eras, such as dresses from the 1950s or shoes from the 1980s. Some designer vintage items, such as Chanel handbags, can be more expensive than new items because of their historic value.

VINYL A type of plastic material that looks smooth like leather and is soft enough to be made into clothes. It was used to make fashionable clothing in the 1960s and 1970s.

WAISTCOAT In the 1500s a waistcoat (now called a vest) was a waist-length coat meant to be worn under a longer coat. Eventually the waistcoat became sleeveless. It is traditionally worn by men as part of a formal suit, but is also worn by women.

WAISTLINE Position of the waist, which on clothing can be above, on, or below the body's natural waist. Fashion designers move the waistline up or down to create different effects.

WEDGE A triangular-shaped high heel on womens' shoes. The modern version of wedge heels was first made in the 1930s by Italian shoe designer Salvatore Ferragamo using lightweight materials such as cork.

WESTERN STYLE The type of clothing worn by cowboys in the western United States, including blue jeans, chunky leather belts, cowboy boots, and cowboy hats. The look was big in fashion in the 1950s and again in the 1990s.

WHALEBONE Not actually a bone but long, hairy strips, or bristles (called baleen), inside the whale's mouth. Because the bristles are flexible yet tough they have been used in fashion since at least the 1600s for stiffening corsets and collars.

WINKLEPICKERS Shoes or boots with long pointed toes. They were part of the outfits worn by rock 'n' roll fans in Britain in the 1950s, and then became part of mainstream fashion, especially among women. The name comes from the sharp tool used for picking molluscs called winkles out of their shells.

WRAPAROUND Any garment that is wrapped around the body and tied on, such as a sarong. Also a classic dress by American designer Diane von Furstenberg; it was wrapped around the body and tied with a belt of the same fabric.

Designer Directory

A list of every influential fashion designer in history could fill an entire book. Instead, here is just a small selection of the names who have helped to shape the way we dress.

GIORGIO ARMANI
Italian Giorgio Armani became a household name in the 1980s, after dressing film star Richard Gere. His key look was a laid-back suit and tasteful colors like beige, gray, and dove blue. The silhouette was lean and relaxed, never too tight.

BALENCIAGA
Spanish-born Cristóbal Balenciaga started selling his sculptural designs in Paris in 1937, and quickly became known as the most innovative designer in the fashion industry. The brand's reputation has continued, with various designers taking on the challenge since the founder's death. It is now most famous for its handbags.

VICTORIA BECKHAM
The British designer first became famous as "Posh Spice," a pop star in the Spice Girls, and then wife of soccer player David Beckham. In 2007 she launched her own denim line, followed by a fully fledged fashion collection with shows at New York

Fashion Week. Her label is known for its fitted dresses and beautiful fabrics.

MANOLO BLAHNIK
Shoe designer to the stars, London-based Manolo is famous for his classic, beautifully made stilettos. He began designing shoes in the 1970s but it was in the 1990s that his stilettos became the must-have footwear of the rich and famous, from Princess Diana to Madonna and Kate Moss. Part of his success is owed to the fact that whenever he designs a new shoe, he first makes it by hand, carving it from wood until the proportions are perfect.

BURBERRY
In 1856, Englishman Thomas Burberry started making waterproof jackets that could be worn for outdoor sports. He couldn't have imagined that one day his label would be attached to a high-fashion range that includes everything from babies' trench coats to women's evening dresses.

CÉLINE
The French house of Céline dates back to 1945, when it was set up as a children's shoe shop, but by 1969 it had developed into a brand making elegant sportswear. The focus on minimal, beautifully made clothes has continued, and in 2008 Phoebe Philo became creative director—helping to make Céline incredibly influential in the fashion world, especially when it comes to shoes and handbags.

CHANEL
The house of Chanel was started by Frenchwoman Gabrielle "Coco" Chanel in the 1920s, introducing a new, more relaxed way of dressing for women. Chanel also pioneered the idea of branding, adding perfume to her fashion line and adopting the now-famous interlocking Cs as her logo. When Karl Lagerfeld started designing for the house of Chanel in 1983, he revived the CC logo and helped to make Chanel one of the most desirable brands on the planet.

CHLOÉ
This French label was started in Paris in 1952 by Gaby Aghion, who had the idea of making luxurious ready-to-wear (*pret-a-porter*) clothes. This was at a time when there was very expensive haute couture at one end of fashion, and cheap copies at the other end, but not much in between. The Chloé brand is famous for soft, comfortable, feminine clothes.

COMMES DES GARCONS
In 1981, Japanese designer Rei Kawakubo brought her label to Paris, and caused a sensation. Like fellow Japanese designer Yohji Yamamoto, Kawakubo showed minimal, all-black collections with experimental shapes, when everyone else was doing glitzy, colorful, and tailored. She now has a fashion empire, and continues to challenge mainstream ideas about beauty and fashion.

CHRISTIAN DIOR
One of the most famous names in fashion, Frenchman Dior founded his company in

1946 and became the most influential designer of the 1950s. He created the silhouette of fitted top, cinched waist, and full, ballerina-style skirt that cemented the trend for most of the decade. The brand made a huge comeback in the 1990s, with John Galliano as head designer. (see dress p.59)

DOLCE & GABBANA

Since 1985 Italian duo Domenico Dolce and Stefano Gabbana have been presenting their collections in Milan, attracting celebrities and supermodels who have become fans of their glamorous, feminine clothes. The design partners have said that their inspiration is the Italian island of Sicily (where Domenico Dolce was born). Their collections often incorporate lingerie details and extravagant patterns.

FENDI

Carla Fendi and her four sisters run the Italian house of Fendi, which was started by their mother in Rome in 1918. Fendi became a huge name in the 1990s, thanks to Karl Lagerfeld, who had been head designer since 1965; he helped launch the "Baguette" bag of 1997, fashion's first cult handbag. The brand is best known for fur and leather.

JEAN PAUL GAULTIER

Known for mixing cultural influences from all over the world, drawing on pop culture, and crossing gender boundaries, French designer Jean Paul Gaultier established his name in Paris in the 1980s. His collections have often been daring and always attention-grabbing. He has created costumes for several movies, and stage outfits for Madonna and Kylie Minogue.

GIVENCHY

Perhaps best known for being Audrey Hepburn's favorite designer in the 1950s and 1960s, Hubert de Givenchy created sharp, modern shapes that were never risky but always looked polished and ladylike. He founded his label in Paris, France, in 1952 and after decades of success finally retired in 1995. Several designers have stepped into his shoes, including John Galliano, Alexander McQueen, and Riccardo Tisci.

GUCCI

Italian luggage-maker Gucci was one of the most popular handbag and accessory brands of the 1950s and 1960s, worn by movie stars such as Audrey Hepburn and society celebrities such as First Lady Jacqueline Kennedy. Gucci's handbags have helped make it the biggest-selling Italian brand.

MARC JACOBS

He was fired from his first big job at American sportswear label Perry Ellis, but from 1994 onward Jacobs became one of the biggest trendsetters in American fashion with his two labels, Marc Jacobs and Marc by Marc Jacobs. His trick was to make upscale versions of the clothes that women really wanted to wear, and that looked just right for that moment in time. Marc Jacobs also helped to revive the French Louis Vuitton brand, working as its head designer from 1997 to 2013.

CHRISTOPHER KANE

Scottish-born brother and sister Christopher and Tammy Kane are the talents behind this label, which began in 2006 with a collection of neon, body-con bandage dresses. The collections have become more sophisticated, but they remain fresh, smart, and very popular with customers.

DONNA KARAN

In the 1980s, US designer Donna Karan introduced a new way of dressing for the working woman—stretchy jersey separates that could be easily mixed and matched. Bodysuits and opaque tights were the basic elements around which she built her simple, minimal collections.

CALVIN KLEIN

This American label started the trend for branded T-shirts back in 1974, when store buyers wanted to stock the CK logo T-shirts worn by staff at runway shows in New York. In the 1970s Calvin Klein became the first high-fashion brand to show jeans with the designer's logo on the pocket. Calvin Klein also launched the first underwear with a designer logo.

MICHAEL KORS

The woman on the Michael Kors catwalk always looks like she is just about to go on vacation—either on a yacht, on the ski slopes, or to a tropical island. Kors mixes the ideas of relaxed, sporty dressing with ladylike luxury, and combines neutral basics with bright shots of color. He has been building the Michael Kors brand since his debut in New York in 1981, and is known around the world for designing classic American sportswear.

LACOSTE

René Lacoste was the world's No. 1 tennis player in 1926–27, but he was also interested in clothes, especially pieces he could wear on the court. He started a fashion company with his personal symbol, the crocodile, as its logo. Lacoste crossed over from sports to fashion in the 1980s when the brand's famous polo shirts were worn as an intregal part of the "preppy" look.

CHRISTIAN LACROIX

Frenchman Lacroix launched his label in 1987, and his extravagant clothes captured the imagination of anyone interested in fashion. He designed both couture and ready-to-wear, and was very successful, but his business closed in 2007. Since then he has freelanced, creating costumes for theater and collections for other design houses.

KARL LAGERFELD

The undisputed king of fashion for the past 50 years, German-born Lagerfeld got his first fashion job as assistant to Pierre Balmain in 1955. He went on to head the label Chloé for almost 20 years, and then took up the top job at Chanel in 1983, even though everyone thought he had no chance of reviving the old label. Of course he did, and managed to make it one of the most successful brands in history. He also designs for Fendi and his own Karl Lagerfeld label, and finds time to direct TV commercials and photograph for the Chanel catalogs.

LANVIN

Frenchwoman Jeanne Lanvin launched her hat-making business in 1889, but it was only after becoming a mother to daughter Marguerite that she decided to expand into children's wear. As her daughter grew, Lanvin added women's clothing, becoming one of the most popular designers of the 1920s and 1930s. Her dresses were always beautifully embellished with beading, embroidery, and trims, a tradition that continues today under head designer Alber Elbaz.

RALPH LAUREN

A Jewish kid from a rough neighborhood in New York, Ralph Lauren decided to create the fantasy of a rich, upper-class lifestyle through fashion, establishing his label in 1971. The next year he launched the now famous polo shirt with the polo player logo embroidered on the upper left-hand side.

CHRISTIAN LOUBOUTIN

The shoe designer whose signature is shiny red soles has made some of the most spectacular stilettos on the red carpet. He had a rocky start, though, dropping out of school at the age of 12 and living in Egypt and India before returning to Paris. Louboutin designed shoes for many big brands before setting up his own business in 1991.

STELLA MCCARTNEY

Despite the supposed advantage of being a daughter of Beatle Paul McCartney, Stella McCartney has proved herself as one of the leading designers to emerge in the 21st century. She designs tailored, comfortable clothes that always have a modern edge, exactly the things she wants to wear herself.

ALEXANDER MCQUEEN

Dramatic, romantic, and extravagant, the clothes designed by Londoner Alexander McQueen always had a dark side—his signature emblem was the skull. The young designer died in 2010 but his spirit lives on in Sarah Burton, who worked closely with McQueen for years and became head designer after his death. Burton famously created the wedding gown for Kate Middleton when she married Prince William in 2011.

MISSONI

The Missoni look is one of the most recognizable in fashion. The Italian brand's signature since 1953 has been finely knitted clothes and accessories in stripes and zigzags, used for dresses, jackets, tops, pants, bikinis, and even shoes and bags. Although the family-run business has changed with the times, designing home furnishings and hotels for example, its devotion to geometric pattern is as strong as ever.

ERDEM MORALIOGLU

He worked for Vivienne Westwood and Diane Von Furstenberg before setting up his own studio in London in 2005. Since then Erdem Moralioglu has won several prestigious fashion prizes, and his dreamy dresses of lace and tulle are sold at major stores around the world.

PRADA

The Prada label started out in 1913, supplying luggage to the Savoy royal family who reigned in Italy at that time. Prada bags are still beautifully made, and expensive, but now there is a huge range of fashion goods produced by the brand, under head designer Miuccia Prada (her grandfather started the business).

SONIA RYKIEL

She has been the stripey knitwear queen of Paris since the 1960s, becoming incredibly popular for her cute striped separates, combined with lots of black, and her vision of cheeky Parisian chic. Her signature look is a shrunken striped sweater with a mini skater skirt.

YVES SAINT LAURENT

This is one of the great names in fashion from the past 50 years. Founder Yves Saint Laurent rose to fame in the 1960s and 1970s as the first designer to present a full ready-to-wear (pret-a-porter) collection. In other words, you could buy it off the rack in stores in set sizes, rather than paying many times more to have it made especially to your measurements (which is what happens in *haute couture*). Saint Laurent's big contributions to fashion were recreating a men's tuxedo for women, and the safari look.

ANNA SUI

Inspired by rock music and art history, New York–based Anna Sui has been a powerful influence in fashion since she started her own business, paying models with clothes in the early days as she struggled to become established. She is known for her colorful prints and fun designs. (see dress p.69)

VALENTINO

The most glamorous of the Italian fashion houses, Valentino's speciality has always been fabulous evening wear, especially red dresses. Valentino Garavani established the label in Rome, Italy, in 1959, with help from his father, designing gowns for princesses, movie stars, and heiresses. Although Valentino himself retired in 2007, his name lives on with a new generation of design talent.

DRIES VAN NOTEN

His grandfather was a tailor and his father sold men's wear, so it is not surprising that Dries Van Noten went into fashion. He started his label in his home city of Antwerp, Belgium, in 1986, and has developed a cult following worldwide for his beautiful layered clothes made from amazing fabrics. Famously, he has never advertised.

VERSACE

Created by Gianni Versace in 1978, and now run by his sister, Donatella, Versace is one of the most glamorous brands in fashion. It mixes the classical styles of Ancient Greece and Rome with rock 'n' roll to create fantasy clothes that look more suited to celebrities and supermodels than to everyday life.

DIANE VON FURSTENBERG

Part of the New York scene from the 1970s onward, Diane Von Furstenberg is most famous for creating one thing—a wraparound, knee-length dress made from stretchy jersey. Her dresses have been worn by many high-profile women including Michelle Obama, Madonna, and Jennifer Lopez.

LOUIS VUITTON

In 1854, a young Frenchman named Louis Vuitton set up a business in Paris making customized luggage. By 1896, he was producing bags and suitcases printed all over with his initials, LV. Fast-forward 120 years and his name is one of the most famous fashion brands (and the most faked) in the world.

ALEXANDER WANG

One of fashion's youngest success stories, Alexander Wang not only had his own label by the age of 22, but several years later was also invited to take up the post of head designer at Balenciaga in Paris. His look is streamlined and sporty and always has a sharp, streetwise edge.

VERA WANG

New Yorker Vera Wang was a figure skater before turning to fashion. She worked at *Vogue* magazine for a few years, and then started to design. In 1989 she founded her wedding gown studio, and has gone on to become the most recognized name in bridal wear, making dresses for socialites and celebrities. She has also designed costumes for champion ice skaters and cheerleaders.

VIVIENNE WESTWOOD

Reinventing history is Vivienne Westwood's passion, and she has been responsible for some of the biggest British looks since the 1970s, including punk fashion, corsets as outerwear, mini crinolines, and mega platform stilettos.

Index

Acknowledgments

The publisher would like to thank the following for their kind permission to reproduce their photographs:

(Key: a-above; b-below/bottom; c-center; f-far; l-left; r-right; t-top)

1 Dorling Kindersley: Judith Miller/Cristobal. **6 Getty Images:** Charles Norfleet/FilmMagic (l/dark blue outfit); Kristy Sparow/WireImage (l/dress & light-blue cardigan); Kirstin Sinclair/FilmMagic (r). **7 Alamy Images:** Paule Saviano/Lebrecht Music & Arts (l/hat, scarf, skirt, bag & shoes). **Corbis:** Fairchild Photo Service/Condé Nast (c). **Getty Images:** PYMCA/Universal Images Group (r/trousers & bag). **8 Getty Images:** Jon Kopaloff/FilmMagic (l); Mercedes-Benz/Frazer Harrison (fcl); Caroline McCredie (r). **9 Getty Images:** Neil P. Mockford/FilmMagic; Daniel Zuchnik (c). **10 Dorling Kindersley:** Ermine Street Guard (br). **12 Corbis:** Bettmann (bc). **Dorling Kindersley:** Ashmolean Museum, Oxford (ca). **Getty Images:** DEA/S. Vannini/De Agostini (r). **13 Alamy Images:** Peter Barritt (tc). **Corbis:** Kevin Schafer (cla). **Dorling Kindersley:** Judith Miller/Ancient Art (c). **Getty Images:** G. Dagli Orti/De Agostini Picture Library (r). **14 Corbis:** The Gallery Collection (cr); Musée Condée, Chantilly, France. Ann Ronan Picture Library/Heritage Images (c). **Getty Images:** Museum of London/The Bridgeman Art Library (bc). **15 Getty Images:** Charles Norfleet/FilmMagic (l). **17 Alamy Images:** Holbein, Hans the Elder (1460/5-1524)/The Art Gallery Collection (c). **The Bridgeman Art Library:** Victoria & Albert Museum, London, UK (r). **18-19 Alamy Images:** Mouse in the House (tc). **Dreamstime.com:** Eyewave (background). **19 Dreamstime.com:** Sofiaworld (br/silkworm); Vladimir Zadvinskii (br/leaf). **20 The Bridgeman Art Library:** Hardwick Hall, Derbyshire, UK/National Trust Photographic Library/P.A. Burton (r); Walker Art Gallery, National Museums Liverpool (bl). **Getty Images:** The Bridgeman Art Library (bc). **21 The Bridgeman Art Library:** Hardwick Hall, Derbyshire, UK/National Trust Photographic Library/P.A. Burton (tr). **Getty Images:** The Bridgeman Art Library (cb). **22 The Bridgeman Art Library:** The Royal Collection © 2014 Her Majesty Queen Elizabeth II (a). **Dreamstime.com:** Sommersby (ca/frame). **23 The Bridgeman Art Library:** Walters Art Museum, Baltimore, USA (r). **24-25 Museum of London:** (dress). **26 Photograph by John Chase:** Olive Matthews Collection, Chertsey Museum (l). **V&A Images/Victoria and Albert Museum, London:** (bl). **27 Photograph by John Chase:** Olive Matthews Collection, Chertsey Museum (cla). **Getty Images:** Jason Merritt (r). **V&A Images/Victoria and Albert Museum, London:** (bl). **Getty Images:** Apic/Hulton Archive (r). **31 Alamy Images:** EP Stock (br). **Corbis:** The Gallery Collection (tr). **Dorling Kindersley:** Worthing Museum and Art Gallery (ca). **Getty Images:** David Cooper/Toronto Star (tl). **32 Corbis:** The Print Collector (br). **33 Alamy Images:** The Print Collector (r). **Getty Images:** G. Dagli Orti/De Agostini (tl). **34 Dorling Kindersley:** Judith Miller/Charlotte Sayers FGA (ftl). **35 Getty Images:** Kristy Sparow/WireImage (l/dress & cardigan). **Dreamstime.com:** Sommersby (bc/frame). **37 Dorling Kindersley:** Judith Miller/Charlotte Sayers FGA (ca); Judith Miller/Sylvie Spectrum (c). **43 Getty Images:** Kirstin Sinclair/FilmMagic (l/jacket, hat, trousers & shoes). **44 The Bridgeman Art Library:** Private Collection (r). **47 Alamy Images:** Peter Barritt/Robert Harding World Imagery (br). **49 Alamy Images:** Paule Saviano/Lebrecht Music & Arts (l/hat, scarf, skirt, bag & shoes). **50 V&A Images/Victoria and Albert Museum, London:** (cb). **51 V&A Images/Victoria and Albert Museum, London:** Given by Messrs Harrods Ltd (bc). **52 V&A Images/Victoria and Albert Museum, London:** (tl). **58 Alamy Images:** JT Vintage Agency/Glasshouse Images (tl, tc). **59 Corbis:** Fairchild Photo Service/Condé Nast (outfit). **60 Dorling Kindersley:** Judith Miller/Marie Antiques (tl). **Photo SCALA, Florence:** The Metropolitan Museum of Art/Art Resource. **63 Getty Images:** PYMCA/Universal Images Group (trousers & bag). **64 Dorling Kindersley:** Judith Miller/Wallis and Wallis (ca); Judith Miller/RBR Group at Grays (bc). **65 Smithsonian**

Institution, Washington, DC, USA: (r). **68 Dorling Kindersley:** Museum of London (cb). **Getty Images:** Mercedes-Benz/Frazer Harrison (l/dress). **70 Dorling Kindersley:** Museum of London (cl); Judith Miller/Eclectica (c); Judith Miller/Junkyard Jeweler (bc). **71 Dorling Kindersley:** Judith Miller/Wallis and Wallis (bl). **73 Dorling Kindersley:** Judith Miller/Cristobal (tr); Judith Miller/Mod-Girl (cra). **Photo SCALA, Florence:** The Metropolitan Museum of Art (tl, bl). **75 Dorling Kindersley:** Judith Miller/Eclectica (clb). **76 Getty Images:** John Kobal Foundation/Moviepix (r). **78 Corbis:** Philadelphia Museum of Art (r). **Dorling Kindersley:** Judith Miller/Roxanne Stuart (tc); Judith Miller/Cristobal (bc). **Photo SCALA, Florence:** The Metropolitan Museum of Art/Art Resource (l). **79 Dorling Kindersley:** Judith Miller/Richard Gibbon (tl). **81 Dorling Kindersley:** Judith Miller/The Design Gallery. **84 Getty Images:** Eggit/Fox Photos/Hulton Archive (r). **The Library of Congress, Washington DC:** LC-USW36-434 (cl). **86 Dorling Kindersley:** Judith Miller/The Design Gallery (br). **87 Getty Images:** Felix Man/Picture Post (r). **88 Getty Images:** Keystone-France/Gamma-Keystone (cr). **89 Getty Images:** Caroline McCredie (l/cardigan, skirt & shoes). **90 Corbis:** Condé Nast Archive/John Rawlings (l). **Dorling Kindersley:** Judith Miller/Cristobal (tr); Judith Miller/William Wain at Antiquarius (c); Judith Miller/Wallis and Wallis (cr, br). **91 V&A Images/Victoria and Albert Museum, London:** (l). **92 Dorling Kindersley:** Judith Miller/William Wain at Antiquarius (cra). **Getty Images:** Mondadori (bl). **92-93 Corbis:** Bettmann (b). **93 Dorling Kindersley:** Judith Miller/William Wain at Antiquarius (b). **Rex Features:** Ken McKay (tr). **94 Dorling Kindersley:** Judith Miller/Cloud Cuckoo Land (tl/dresses); Judith Miller/Sparkle Moore at The Girl Can't Help It (br/sunglasses & shoe); Judith Miller/Cristobal (bc). **95 Dorling Kindersley:** Judith Miller/Cloud Cuckoo Land (clb); Judith Miller/Wallis and Wallis (bl); Judith Miller/Richard Gibbon (tc). **97 Getty Images:** RDA/Hulton Archive. **98-99 Dreamstime.com:** Raja Rc (background). **98 Dreamstime.com:** Denis Babenko (bl); Travisowenby (tr/leather tag). **National Air and Space Museum, Smithsonian Institution:** (tr/Amelia Earhart). **99 Dreamstime.com:** Supertrooper (br). **100 Corbis:** William Gottlieb (r); John Springer Collection (cla). **102 Dorling Kindersley:** Judith Miller/Sparkle Moore at The Girl Can't Help It (tl/sunglasses); Judith Miller/Wallis and Wallis (cl); Judith Miller/Cloud Cuckoo Land (bl/skirts). **Getty Images:** Popperfoto (r). **103 Getty Images:** Popperfoto (tr). **TopFoto.co.uk:** Ken Russel (bl). **104 Getty Images:** Popperfoto (r, bl). **105 Dorling Kindersley:** Judith Miller/Barbara Blau (r); Judith Miller/Mary Ann's Collectibles (cla); Judith Miller/Wallis and Wallis (crb); Judith Miller/Steinberg and Tolkien (br). **112 Dreamstime.com:** Clipart Design (man on horse). **V&A Images/Victoria and Albert Museum, London:** (tc); (bl). **106 Dorling Kindersley:** Judith Miller/Wallis and Wallis (tl); Judith Miller/Linda Bee (cl/black & red necklace); Judith Miller/Freeman's (bc); Judith Miller (fcl). **V&A Images/Victoria and Albert Museum, London:** (br). **107 Corbis:** Condé Nast Archive/Marc Hispard (r). **108 Dorling Kindersley:** Judith Miller/Wallis and Wallis (tc). **109 Corbis:** Steve Schapiro (r). **Dorling Kindersley:** Judith Miller/Wallis and Wallis (bl). **110 Corbis:** Condé Nast Archive (bl). **Dorling Kindersley:** Judith Miller/Linda Bee (tc). **Getty Images:** Manchester Daily Express/SSPL/Hulton Archive (cr). **111 Getty Images:** Daniel Zuchnik (l/top, trousers & bag). **112 Dreamstime.com:** Clipart Design (man on horse); Tuja66 (cra/rivets); Flas100 (clb). **113 Dorling Kindersley:** The Science Museum, London (br). **Dreamstime.com:** Rasslava (tr/zip); Tuja66 (tr/buttons). **114 LGI Stock** (clb). **Getty Images:** Michael Putland/Hulton Archive (br). **115 Alamy Images:** Mario Mitsis (tl). **Pearson Asset Library:** Pearson Education Asia Ltd/Coleman Yuen (tr/skirt). **116 Alamy Images:** AF archive/Paramount (cr). **Dorling Kindersley:** Judith Miller/Linda Bee (bl); Judith Miller/Wallis and Wallis (tc). **Getty Images:** Aaron Davidson (br); Harry Langdon/Archive Photos (cl). **117 Corbis:** Condé Nast Archive/Denis Piel (r). **Dorling Kindersley:** Judith Miller/Million Dollar Babies (tl); Judith Miller/Linda Bee (ca). **Getty Images:** Carl Juste/Miami Herald/McClatchy-Tribune

(cl). **118 Dorling Kindersley:** Judith Miller/Wallis and Wallis (clb, cb, bl, bc); Judith Miller/Fantiques (crb); Judith Miller/Antique Textiles and Lighting (tl, tc); Judith Miller/Linda Bee (br). **119 Alamy Images:** Peter Horree (bc). **Dorling Kindersley:** Judith Miller/Cheffins (tl); Judith Miller/Bonny Yankauer (tc); Judith Miller/Richard Gibbon (tr); Judith Miller/Wallis and Wallis (cl, cr); Judith Miller/Sara Covelli (c). **Getty Images:** Carl Juste/Miami Herald/McClatchy-Tribune (bl); Pool/Benainous/Catarina/Legrand/Gamma-Rapho (br). **120 Corbis:** Mauro Carraro/Sygma (cr); Condé Nast Archive (l). **121 Getty Images:** Neil P. Mockford/FilmMagic (l/outfit). **122 Alamy Images:** Peter Horree (bc). **Corbis:** Condé Nast Archive (l). **Photo SCALA, Florence:** The Metropolitan Museum of Art (br). **123 Photo SCALA, Florence:** The Metropolitan Museum of Art (cb); The Metropolitan Museum of Art/Art Resource (r). **126 Corbis:** Philippe Wojazer/Reuters (cla, ca, cra, bl, bc, br). **127 Corbis:** Gonzalo Fuentes/Reuters (bc); Philippe Wojazer/Reuters (cla, ca, cra, bl, br). **128 Getty Images:** Fred Duval/FilmMagic (bl); Neil Mockford/FilmMagic (r). **129 Corbis:** Dylan Martinez/Reuters (r). **134 Getty Images:** Stephen Lovekin (r). **135 Alamy Images:** ZUMA Press, Inc. (tc, tr). **Getty Images:** Fernanda Calfat/CuteCircuit (cr/plain skirt, fcr); Antonio de Moraes Barros Filho/WireImage (bl).

All other images © Dorling Kindersley
For further information see: www.dkimages.com

The publisher would also like to thank the following companies and individuals for their generosity in providing images or allowing photography of their exhibits, private collections and products: Angels the Costumiers & Angels Fancy Dress, www.angels.uk.com; Banbury Museum, www.banburymuseum.org; The Blandford Fashion Museum, www.theblandfordfashionmuseum.co.uk; Central Saint Martins College of Art and Design, www.csm.arts.ac.uk. Reconstruction of Doublet and hose and Cote-hardie on p.16 – Sarah Thursfield The Medieval Tailor, www.sarahthursfield.com; Shoes on p.40 and cover top left and spine – Camilla Elphick www.camillaelphick.com; Jacket on p.49 and cover – Sirens and Starlets www.sirensandstarlets.co.uk; Rockabilly dress on p.101 and cover – Dress 190, http://stores.ebay.co.uk/dress190; Charm Bracelet p.103 – Andrew Moyer, Ken's Collectibles, http://stores.ebay.com/KENS-COLLECTIBLES-OR-ESTATE-JEWELRY; Braclet p.134 – photos by Michael Higgins for Cuff, Inc, www.cuff.io; Fitness trackers p. 134 – Mis fit, www.misfitwearables.com; Sweater p.134 copyright SENSOREE, GER Mood Sweater, design by Kristin Neidlinger sensoree.com; 3D Shoe p.135 – Designed by Janina Alleyne, 3D Modelled by INNER LEAF & 3D Printed by Shapeways; boot p.135 – ANASTASIA RADEVICH, www.anastasiaradevich.com

Dorling Kindersley would like to thank the following people for their help in the preparation of this book: Margaret McCormack for Indexing, Debra Wolter for Proofreading, Katie John for Glossary Illustrations, Rhiannon Carroll for Modeling, Adam Brackenbury for Creative Support, Andrew Scott Taylor for help with fashion terminology

The publisher would like to thank the following people from the London College of Fashion for their involvement in the My Life pages: Camilla Elphick BA (Hons) Cordwainers Footwear: Product Design and Innovation, Barbra Kolasinski MA Fashion Design Technology Womenswear, Flora Robson and Poppy Kenny BA (Hons) Hair and Make-up for Fashion, Lynsey Fox Acting Media Relations Manager, Sue Saunders Course Director BA (Hons) Cordwainers Footwear: Product Design and Innovation, Nigel Luck Course Director of MA Fashion Technology: Womenswear

The author would like to thank her daughter Daisy Nicholls for patiently reading every word of the book, even during homework time.